From

Wilderness

To

Worship

By Cheryl Gerou

From Wilderness to Worship
Copyright ©2011 by Cheryl Gerou
Cover designed by Cheryl Gerou
Published by C. Gerou

ISBN 978-0-615-57410-3
Second Edition

DEDICATION:

In loving memory of my paternal grandfather, "Opah,"
Rev. Frederic Otto Marohn (1892-1969).
Opah showed me Jesus by the way he
loved me and by the way he lived his life.

A prayer Opah taught me as a child:

"Ich bin klein
Mein Herz mach rein,
Soll neimand drin wohnen,
Als Jesus allein!
Amen!"

Translated:

I am small,
Make my heart clean,
So no one can enter,
But Jesus alone!
Amen!

ACKNOWLEDGMENTS

Frederic and Marilyn Marohn, my dear parents, thank you for encouraging me in my walk with the Lord. Thank you for encouraging me in writing this book. Thank you for reading through it at its very beginnings and pushing me forward to continue to work on it. Thank you for your love and prayers along life's way.

James B. Robar, my editor, thank you for teaching me so much about writing. Thank you for going over it word-by-word and page-by-page to help throughout the process and bring it to completion. This book would have remained in very rough stages without your help.

Delores Liesner, my copy editor, thank you for your time and expertise in polishing my book. The information and ideas you shared have been very helpful in encouraging me to become a better writer. You are a blessing and an answer to prayer.

Thank you to Bob, my husband, for your faithfulness and love throughout our journey together.

Contents

Preface

Life is a journey, different for each one of us. The Lord uses various circumstances in each of our lives to draw us to Him. This book is about my journey with the Lord. I share some of the pitfalls and pain as well as the way I was brought through those times and how the Lord uses them. As I look at my life, so far, I see how the Lord has not wasted anything that He has allowed. He has touched my heart in deep ways both by the hurt and in the joys. He has made Himself real to me in amazing ways.

The words of this book had their start as bits and pieces from my prayer journal, portions of retreats I shared at my church and poems written to sort out deep feelings that seemed too overwhelming.

Each chapter is themed by a verse or portion of a verse from Psalm 23. It is in the themes of this beautiful Psalm of David that I share the Lord's work in my life.

As you read the words of this book and take time to study and answer the questions at the end of each chapter, my prayer is that you will ponder God's presence in each moment. May you see, know, and respond to His lovingkindness with worship in your heart and in your life.

May the Lord hold you in His love,
Cheryl Gerou

How This Book is Organized

The chapters are divided into sections. The purpose of each section follows:

Digging Deeper and Defining

This section gives explanation and definition of words or terms found in or related to the themes of Psalm 23.

The Lord's Word/The Lord's Work

This section provides a deeper look into the scriptures; the truths of His Word, and the work of the Lord in the lives of His people.

My Life Experience

This section gives examples from my personal life, times of personal difficulties or learning experiences that have helped me to grow in my walk with the Lord.

Reaching

This section provides examples and descriptions of spiritual disciplines. These are practices that have proved helpful to me in my daily walk with the Lord as I reach for Him through my ups and downs in life.

Questions for Life Application

This section provides a list of questions that help in personal application. The questions can also be used as mentoring tools in sharing with others how the Lord has brought you personally from wilderness to worship.

Psalm 23

A Psalm of David

1 The LORD is my shepherd; I shall not want.

2 He makes me lie down in green pastures. He leads me beside still waters.

3 He restores my soul. He leads me in paths of righteousness for his name's sake.

4 Even though I walk through the valley of the shadow of death, I will fear no evil, for you are with me; your rod and your staff, they comfort me.

5 You prepare a table before me in the presence of my enemies; you anoint my head with oil; my cup overflows.

6 Surely goodness and mercy shall follow me all the days of my life, and I shall dwell in the house of the LORD forever.

ESV (English Standard Version)

Chapter 1

Knowing the Shepherd,
Being the Sheep

Psalm 23:1-2 (ESV) "The LORD is my shepherd, I shall not want. He makes me lie down in green pastures. He leads me beside still waters."

"The LORD is my Shepherd..."

"The LORD is my Shepherd," is a statement that describes intimate belonging, a sense of having a place with a leader, and in this case a spiritual leader. This little phrase, *The LORD is my Shepherd,* makes it evident that David knew the LORD and trusted in His care. People often use the phrase "I know him/her" in a rather casual way. But belonging and trusting are not part of a casual acquaintance. A shepherd's relationship to his sheep is one

1

of intensive and diligent care. The sheep's life depends on the shepherd's care. Truly "knowing" only comes about in a heart-to-heart, in-depth relationship. Time well spent results in the shepherd and sheep bonding.

Let's become a little better acquainted with both shepherd and sheep, for in doing so we will learn a lot about our relationship as sheep with our Shepherd.

Learning what sheep are like and what the job of the shepherd entailed was very helpful to me in better understanding Psalm 23.

Digging Deeper and Defining:
The Shepherd and His Sheep

It is intriguing that David, a shepherd himself, would call the LORD his Shepherd and himself a sheep. David was very familiar with what weak, defenseless, and foolish animals sheep were, after spending endless hours with them. He too must have realized his own weaknesses.

A shepherd has many responsibilities in caring for his sheep. The shepherd must find safe places for the sheep to drink and graze each day. Finding pasture was difficult for shepherds because the land was dry and water was frequently in short supply. The shepherd needed to make himself familiar with the places he took his flock. The shepherd was responsible for keeping his flock safe.

The terrain of the land was reason for concern due to its many cliffs and deep ravines where the sheep could fall. The sheep could be injured or even die.

Sheep are defenseless animals. David tells of how he, himself, would go after a lion or bear that would take a lamb from the flock. He says that he would rescue the lamb from the enemy's mouth, and at times had to kill both lions and bears in order to keep his flock safe (1 Samuel 17:31-36). A shepherd had to be prepared to protect both himself and his flock. To help in protecting himself and the sheep, he would carry a rod and a staff. The rod was usually a three-foot club the shepherd carried on his belt. This was the shepherd's instrument of defense against wild animals and robbers. The staff was a long stick that had a large curved hook on one end. The shepherd would use this to pull back any straying sheep.

Sheep differ in nature; some are gentle and willingly obedient, while others will linger in a spot or stray off without thought. If a sheep were to stray, the shepherd would relentlessly look for it until he found it. Many times the shepherd would need to put his own life on the line to rescue the stray. If a little lamb was not strong enough to keep up with the rest of the flock, the shepherd would carry it, sometimes carrying more than one. There were many dangers making it necessary for the shepherd to carefully watch the flock at every moment.

Throughout the day and night, the shepherd talked to his

sheep, just as we talk to our pets. The sheep would come to know the voice of the shepherd. The sheep's knowledge of the shepherd's voice was evident when more than one flock were to intermingle while grazing. When it was time to leave, each shepherd would call from a different place in the field to gather his flock. Each shepherd had a specific and somewhat unusual call. When the sheep heard their shepherd call they would respond by moving towards him, so each flock would separate to follow their shepherd.

Each night the shepherd would bring the flock together to go into the fold. The fold was a large circular area made with clumped together stones or bushes. The sheep would enter the fold in single file as the shepherd checked each one for injuries. When all the sheep were inside, the shepherd would guard the entrance by lying down in front of it like a door, protecting the sheep.

As I learned about sheep and shepherds, I began to see how similar I am to a sheep. I am in desperate need for all the Lord has to offer me. I need His leading so that I may walk on His safe path. I must live dependently on Him. Too often, I find myself fretting and fighting for what I need when He has already done it all for me. I need to know His voice in order to follow Him, so that I don't lose my way. I need to know and feel His presence each moment to give me peace. It is just too easy for me to get lost, hungry, or tired and end up in dangerous places in this world where I can feel apart from my Shepherd. It is evident that David saw the Lord as his Shepherd for these same reasons. David knew how he met the needs of the sheep and protected them. In addition, he knew how the Lord met his needs, protecting him as well. David remembered risking his life for the life of a single sheep. The Lord has done the same for us. "All of us like sheep have gone astray, Each of us has turned to his own way; But the LORD has caused the iniquity of us all To fall on Him" (Isaiah 53:6). The danger of hell is our ultimate path's end if we don't walk with the Shepherd.

The Lord our Shepherd delights in giving us all we need, so we might find contentment and rest. We can fully depend upon His loving guidance in knowing He is always with us. Isaiah tells us "Like a shepherd He will tend His flock, In His arm He will gather the lambs And carry *them* in His bosom; He will gently lead the nursing *ewes*" (Isaiah 40:11). This verse speaks of the care of our Lord for His people. We are very much like sheep and how privileged we are to be able to call the Lord, our Shepherd. *The LORD is my Shepherd.* He is our Good Shepherd, leading, guiding, protecting, feeding, nurturing, and keeping us out of harm's way. He laid down His life for us and it is in Him we find true rest and contentment.

The Lord's Word/The Lord's Work:
Trusting in Our Shepherd

"…I shall not want."

I shall not want is a statement that describes true satisfaction and contentment. When I am in want of something, I feel that "want" constantly and it distracts me from what is really important. David is saying because the LORD is his Shepherd, David is not in want of anything. He is fully satisfied, and completely content.

Contentment seems to be something everyone seeks, but struggles to find. So often it is sought in harmful places. It is very difficult to stop the rat race, to find relief, to find rest when our lives are often chaotic with busyness. Therefore, we seek to find contentment by dulling our pain or running after a person or thing that we hope will fill our emptiness.

Jesus calls to us in Matthew 11:28 saying "Come to Me, all who are weary and heavy-laden, and I will give you rest". When we look at the life of Jesus, we see that He was fully dependent on His Father, seeking Him in prayer often (Luke 3:21; 5:16; 6:12; 9:18; 9:28).

Jesus fully desired to do the Father's will and in walking in His will, He was able to walk in rest. He lived His life walking by faith, totally surrendered and trusting in His Father. He didn't fret and worry. Jesus knew something that we often forget. He tells us, "…your Father knows what you need before you ask Him." (Matthew 6:8). Living in trust demonstrates realization of the Lord's knowledge of our needs and our willingness to depend on Him in our neediness. The psalmist tells us to "Rest in the LORD and wait patiently for Him" (Psalm 37:7). Jesus prayed knowing the faithfulness of the Father and this left Him walking in perfect peace.

The apostle Paul seems to have also found the secret of contentment and spells it out for us when he says:

> "…I have learned to be content in whatever circumstances I am. I know how to get along with humble means, and I also know how to live in prosperity; in any and every circumstance I have learned the secret of being filled and going hungry, both of having abundance and suffering need." (Philippians 4:11-12)

Paul speaks of being content whatever circumstances he is enduring. *Content* is defined as, to not need any assistance from the outside. Paul understood the sufficiency that he had in God and he trusted fully in this.

When looking at the circumstances of Paul's life, it is quickly obvious that he did not have an easy life, and his contentment was not without challenge. His life included: attacks, beatings, imprisonment, being put in dungeons, having his feet put in stocks, being spoken evil to and about, disappointment with

people who were stubborn in their attitude to what Paul was
teaching, being weighed down and crushed to the point of
despairing of life, having no rest, being in contention with others,
being afflicted, going hungry, being thirsty, cold, and lacking
clothing.

We learn of Paul's suffering in 2 Corinthians 11:16-33. He
dealt with all of this and still said he knew the secret of
contentment. He knew the Lord, the only One who could provide
that contentment. Psalm 23 keeps bringing us back to the
realization that rest and contentment are only found in knowing
and trusting the Shepherd.

Reaching:
To Find Contentment in Him

It sounds so easy, yet it seems that people search endlessly
trying to figure out how to grasp hold of contentment and it, like a
butterfly, always seems to elude our grasp. Even when I know
what I need, it is hard to stay focused and hold on. I often have to
wonder, do I really know the Shepherd that David speaks of in
Psalm 23? What will it take to get me to that place to be able to say
like David "I shall not want"?

"Whom have I in heaven *but You?* And besides You, I desire
nothing on earth. My flesh and my heart may fail, But God is the

strength of my heart and my portion forever" (Psalm 73:25-26). This is a verse my aunt, Paulette, shared with me around a time in my life when I was seeking belonging and love, and felt incredible discontent. Her hope was that it would touch my heart as it did hers. Paulette has a deeply committed love relationship with the Lord. She has endured many trials and many painful circumstances in her life, but through them, she has learned the sufficiency of Christ. She understood the truth of this verse and shared it with me, thinking that it would be helpful to me in a time when I was enduring much pain. I struggled with really understanding what it meant for me. I could not see how the Lord could ever fill all of the emptiness. I thought that I would never really understand the way she did. But, in time, the Lord took me through great learning experiences to teach me more of Who He is and drawing me to truly desire Him.

"He makes me lie down in green pastures; He leads me beside still waters."

David tells us that the Shepherd makes him to *lie down in green pastures* and He leads *beside still waters*. In green pastures I am filled, I am not left hungry. Beside still and restful waters I have a place to drink and my thirst is quenched. I have no need to fear. It is a peaceful place where He meets my needs, a place where I can truly rest. He demonstrates His sufficiency. He satisfies me. The green pastures and still waters aren't a place on a map in this life. They are a place in my heart of really, truly knowing the Lord. Life on this earth is not and never will be perfect. There are times of contentment but they are fleeting. It is very hard to rest when hungering or thirsting after something or other. We read "Blessed are those who hunger and thirst for righteousness, for they shall be satisfied" (Matthew 5:6). Our hunger and thirst can be fully quenched in Jesus, in who He is. Jesus tells us:

> "For the Bread of God is He Who comes down out of heaven and gives life to the world. Then they said to Him, Lord, give us this bread always (all the time)! Jesus replied, I am the Bread of Life. He who comes to Me will never be hungry, and he who believes in *and* cleaves to *and* trusts in *and* relies on Me will never thirst any more (at any time)." (John 6:33-35 AMP)

I have found this to be true when I choose to feed on His faithfulness.

In reality, what it really comes down to is asking our self, "Is knowing the Lord enough?" In Genesis 22:1-8, God asks Abraham to sacrifice Isaac, his long promised son. Isaac is to make Abraham the father of nations. And yet, God asks Abraham to kill him. Why? In a sense, Abraham is being asked a question that the Lord poses to us through many of life's problems. That question is, "Am I enough?"

Amy Carmichael, missionary to India, at one point in her life was very sick and confined to her bed. It was at that time that someone she had hoped to see from her fellowship came to her village. He was on furlough and she had her heart set on being able to greet him. She prayed about this, yet her health did not improve, so she was confined to her bed and unable to go see him. In the midst of her disappointment, this little song filled her heart:

"Thou hast not that, My child, but Thou hast Me,
And am not I alone enough for thee?
I know it all, know how thy heart was set
Upon this joy which is not given yet.

And well I know how through the wistful days
Thou walkest all the dear familiar ways,
As unregarded as a breath of air,
But there in love and longing, always there.

I know it all; but from thy brier shall blow
A rose for others, If it were not so
I would have told thee. Come then, say to Me
My Lord, my Love, I am content with Thee.[1]

Amy was learning of the contentment that she could find in the Lord. I, too, want to learn that. I am learning more and more about finding contentment as I learn to abide in the Lord's love described in this verse, "How precious is Your steadfast love, O

---

[1] Carmichael, Amy <u>Rose From Brier,</u> Christian Literature Crusade,1972 p.52

God! The children of men take refuge *and* put their trust under the shadow of Your wings. They relish *and* feast on the abundance of Your house; and You cause them to drink of the stream of Your pleasures" Psalm 36:7-8 (AMP). The goodness of God is something to be enjoyed. Under the shadow of His wing we are protected, our needs are met, we are fed, and given drink. In addition, all of this comes from His unending love. Under the shadow of His wing, we can find rest, we are strengthened, and we are restored. His grace is sufficient and in His sufficiency I am led to learn of contentment.

Recently a friend was in a similar place as I had been, not really understanding what it means to desire God. She wanted something that she couldn't have, and her prayer for it wasn't being answered as she had hoped. I didn't even know what to say to her when she asked what it really meant to desire God, what that really looked like. I didn't give her an immediate answer. I told her that I needed to think about it in order to explain it. I thought about it as I went through my day. Later I sat down and wrote the following in my journal, what it really meant to me to desire God.

To me desiring God means:
To desire His Presence in and with me
To desire to know His love in all of its fullness
To desire to know His truths for me and my life
To desire His wisdom for each moment of every day
To desire His perfect will for my life because I know in that I

12

will be content and satisfied.
To desire to know the fullness of the attributes of His
character and to feed on that in this life.

While it is easily said to desire God in all moments of life,
Satan would have it otherwise. I have found that Satan often so
easily deceives me into believing that I would be so much better
off in wanting something different, something apart from truly
desiring the Lord and His will for me. Let's look at some contrasts
between where Satan seeks to lead us and what the Lord desires
for us. As you read them consider if you find them true in your
life.

- *Satan draws our attention constantly to our neediness, our
  pain.*

Jesus draws our attention to His sufficiency. All of our needs are
met in His grace. The apostle Paul is told, "My grace is sufficient
for you, for power is perfected in weakness" (2 Corinthians 12:9).

- *Satan draws our attention to our hunger, thirst and
  emptiness.*

Jesus leads us to know Him as the bread of life and He offers us living water. He alone nourishes and quenches all hunger and thirst. He alone fills our emptiness. Jesus promises "I am the bread of life; he who comes to Me will not hunger, and he who believes in Me will never thirst." (John 6:35).

- *Satan draws our attention to our loneliness and offers illegitimate sex and worldly love.*

Jesus is God's gift of love to us. Jesus will never leave us or forsake us. The Scriptures tell us, *"Make sure that* your character is free from the love of money, being content with what you have; for He Himself has said, I WILL NEVER DESERT YOU, NOR WILL I EVER FORSAKE YOU" (Hebrews 13:5).

- *Satan can only tell us lies; he is the deceiver, the father of lies.*

Jesus offers us the Spirit of truth, when He says, "When the Helper comes, whom I will send to you from the Father, *that is* the Spirit of truth who proceeds from the Father, He will testify about Me . . . " (John 15:26).

- *Satan tries to devour us in shame, dissatisfaction, depression, and bitterness. Satan only offers us death.*

Jesus offers us life through the cross. "This righteousness from God comes through faith in Jesus Christ to all who believe…" Romans 3:22 (NIV).

It all comes back to trust. Who will you trust? Who can you rest in? Who shepherds your heart?

Paul tells us that God's grace is sufficient for whatever state we are in. His love is full, His mercy abounds, and therefore I can be content because I have all I need in Jesus. He is the ever-present source of all I need. Satisfaction in Him is my only means of contentment.

My Life Experience: Wandering Like a Sheep

Yes, satisfaction in Him is my only means of true contentment, but because I don't continually abide in Him I lack consistent contentment. There often seems to be a place within me that wants more, or wants something better than what I already have. I feel unsettled, I feel unhappy, and I don't want what I have. Whether that is food, clothes, house, car, a different body, a relationship, whatever it is, somehow I have seen greener grass, something more attractive because it appeals to the senses, tempts me and I am pulled to fill the emptiness within by getting what I see, or have seen. I have done that, I get something to fill the emptiness and it does for a while, but soon the emptiness is back.

I also have, on other occasions, felt that discontent inside, the wanting of what seems to elude me, and in feeling that, I have taken those feelings to the Lord. I have told Him about my emptiness, the wanting, I have pleaded with Him to give me what I want. And sometimes He does. However, oftentimes, more likely than not, He reminds me of His faithfulness. He reminds me of how He satisfies me as I come to know Him more.

I am learning that "filling up" doesn't necessarily mean contentment for me. The more I eat, or the more I buy or the more I have, does not equal contentment. The want that we feel within can be for most anything, it may be for good health, or for a child, or for a husband. These areas in life seem to mean even bigger empty spaces. No matter what the empty space within is, somehow it seems insatiable, whatever it is. However, when I finally have it, it seems there always is something else I want.

The Scriptures tell us "...for the joy of the LORD is your strength" (Nehemiah 8:10). When I know the joy of God's presence, when I live in the joy of relationship with Jesus, when I have the joy of abiding with my Sweet Abba, it is then I have the strength to say " no" to the wants that can be filled by things in this world, or by using people in unhealthy ways. When I see that what the Shepherd offers is best, this *sheep* can stop straying and be content in the *pastures* or by the *waters* where the Shepherd takes me.

When I am distant from the Lord, when I am looking to fill my belly of wanting with what the world offers rather than fill my heart with the love Jesus offers, I can be sure that I will remain feeling discontented. In this world of "shopportunities," it seems that there is always one more thing I have to have, but when I know the Lord as my Shepherd and continually seek to know Him more as the One Who leads and guides me, I find I have no wants. He truly satisfies and I can say with David, *the LORD is my Shepherd, I shall not want.*

Questions:
For Life Application:

How does this really matter to your life?

Use the following questions to help you share your heart, as you mentor, or as questions, to ask as you journal your response to this chapter.

1. What are the area(s) in your life that you have difficulty trusting the Lord? What steps can you take to help you get to know the Lord better?

2. How do you think contentment is related to trust? What can you identify as ways in your life that you have tried to find contentment? Were you led into a deeper relationship with the Lord?

3. As you think about whether or not God seems like He is enough, can you name times when it feels like He has been? Are there times in your life when it really feels like He hasn't been?

4. What attribute of God do you think is lacking in your life, leading you to feelings of discontentment?

5. What distracts you from abiding in Him? Of those things that distract you, do you want more of what those have to offer than Him?

6. Reread Amy Carmichael's poem in the chapter. Have you found the Lord to be enough?

Chapter 2

He Restores My Soul

Psalm 23:3 (ESV) "He restores my soul…"

David knows the contentment he found in his relationship with the Shepherd. Verse three tells of the soul restoration found in Christ. Often when reading this Psalm we read over it quickly because of its familiarity and give little regard to this promise of soul restoration. Do you wonder what it really means for you? Would you like to know how it is relevant to you? In order to understand this we must first look at the definition of soul.

Digging Deeper and Defining:
Biblical Usage of Soul

Genesis 2:7 (KJV) helps us begin to understand the meaning of soul. It says, "The LORD God formed man of the dust of the ground, and breathed into his nostrils the breath of life; and man became a living soul." Here we are told that God did not give man a soul, but rather man became a soul when God combined the body with the breath of life. The spirit is the breath of life, which God gave us. Apostle Paul in 1 Thessalonians 5:23 (KJV) says, "And the very God of peace sanctify you wholly; and *I pray* God your whole spirit and soul and body be preserved blameless unto the coming of our Lord Jesus Christ." Here we find that we are made up of three parts: spirit, soul, and body. John Calvin explains that this verse is written:

> …that we may know what the *sanctification of the whole man* is, when he is kept *entire*, or pure, and unpolluted, in spirit, soul, and body, until the day of Christ.[2]

We are continually fully in need of restoration. The sanctification process is ongoing throughout our lives. *He restores my soul.*

John Gill explains that:

> The soul may include the will and affections, which are influenced by the understanding; and in a regenerate man the will is brought to a resignation to the will of God, and the affections are set upon divine things, and the body is the

---

[2] Calvin, John, "Commentary on Philippians, Colossians, and Thessalonians" John Calvin's "Commentary on Philippians, Colossians, and Thessalonians is public domain. .http://www.ccel.org/ccel/calvin/calcom42.vi.vii.v.html

instrument of performing religious and spiritual exercises; and these the apostle prays may be preserved blameless; [3]

Isaiah says in Isaiah 26:9 (KJV) "With my soul have I desired thee in the night; yea, with my spirit within me I seek thee early..." John Calvin in his Commentary on Philippians, Colossians, and Thessalonians says that in this verse. Isaiah is speaking "of his understanding and affection." Calvin goes on to say,

> "For how is the whole man *entire*, except when his thoughts are pure and holy, when all his affections are right and properly regulated, when, in fine, the body itself lays out its endeavors and services only in good works? For the faculty of understanding is held by philosophers to be, as it were, a mistress; the affections occupy a middle place for commanding; the body renders obedience. We see now how well everything corresponds. For then is the man pure and entire, when he thinks nothing in his mind, desires nothing in his heart, does nothing with his body, except what is approved by God. As, however, Paul in this manner commits to God the keeping of the whole man, and all its parts, we must infer from this that we are exposed to innumerable dangers, unless we are protected by his guardianship."[4]

---

[3] John Gill's Exposition of the Bible is in the public domain and may be freely used and distributed. Found at http://www.biblestudytools.com/commentaries/gills-exposition-of -the bible//1-thessalonians-5-23.html

[4] Calvin, John, "Commentary on Philippians, Colossians, and Thessalonians", John Calvin's "Commentary on Philippians, Colossians, and Thessalonians" is public domain. http://www.ccel.org/ccel/calvin/calclm42.vi.vii.v.html

In the midst of all the attacks on the whole me, He (God) is the one who guards and protects me.

He restores my soul. The Hebrew word "shuwb" is the word translated as "restore," in Psalm 23:3. The word "shuwb" is often defined as "to return, turn back."[5] He makes my soul to be just as if I had never sinned.

The word "restore" in the English language has synonyms such as renew, refresh, rejuvenate, redeem, and rescue. So, He *restores my soul* can be restated as He refreshes, He delivers, He rescues, He redeems my vital existence.

The Lord's Word/ The Lord's Work: Soul Condition/Soul Restoration

We find many soul conditions in the Scriptures. Psalm 107:9 (KJV) says, "For He satisfieth the longing soul and filleth the hungry soul with goodness." And Jeremiah 31:25 (AMP) says, "For I will [fully] satisfy the weary soul and I will replenish every languishing and sorrowful person." Within just these two verses,

---

[5]The Old Testament Hebrew Lexicon is Brown, Driver, Briggs, Gesenius Lexicon; this is keyed to the Theological Word Book of the Old Testament." These files are considered public domain.
   Brown, Driver, Briggs and Gesenius. "Hebrew Lexicon entry for Shuwb". "The Old Testament Hebrew Lexicon".
http://www.studylight.org/lex/heb/view.cgi?number=7725

we see five soul conditions described: hungry, languishing, weary, longing, and sorrowful. Hunger speaks of yearning, and thirst. Languishing can be listless, spiritless, weakened, debilitated, or lacking in energy. Weary is synonymous with fatigue, being oppressed, and even depressed. Longing can be rendered as strong desire or craving. And finally, sorrowful has the same meaning as grieving, heartache, anguish, distress, regret, suffering, or dejection. On any given day, life circumstances can inundate us with any number of these conditions. Suddenly, *He restores my soul* becomes more relevant to our day-to-day existence.

The Gospel tells us of God's restoration plan through Christ's death and resurrection leading to our salvation through our faith, which is also a gift from God. (Eph. 2:8-9) God has restored us back to Himself, since the original fall into sin in the Garden of Eden, through Christ. But, it is clear as we consider the conditions of the soul, that soul restoration is ongoing in life.

Psalm 107:9 promises that God will satisfy and Jeremiah 31:25 promises that He will satisfy and replenish. Satisfaction and replenishment are exactly what the languishing, weary, longing, hungry, or sorrowful soul needs. But, how are these promises made real? Men and women of the Bible experienced these conditions of the soul. These promises were for them, as they are for us. Let's look at three scriptural examples:

In 1 Samuel 1:10 (KJV) we have the story of Hannah. Dealing with infertility, she was in "bitterness of soul." We are told that she "prayed unto the Lord and wept sore." Eli, the priest, misinterpreted Hannah's prayer; he accused her of being drunk. She responded by telling him, "No my lord, I am a woman oppressed in spirit, I have drunk neither wine nor strong drink, but have poured out my soul before the LORD" (1 Samuel 1:15 (KJV)).

In Job 7:11 (KJV), we find Job saying, "Therefore I will not restrain my mouth; I will speak in the anguish of my spirit, I will complain in the bitterness of my soul." Job was afflicted by all of the losses incurred, physical pain and suffering, and being attacked by Satan.

In Psalm 6:3 it states that David was "sore vexed" (KJV) or "greatly dismayed". Throughout David's life he often found himself in danger, due to war, enemies, or trouble in family relationships, all due to sin. The many Psalms that he wrote cry out to the Lord often because of difficulties in his life.

Each of these people, Hannah, Job, and David all cried out complaining, praying, and questioning the Lord. The Lord promises to satisfy, to fill, to replenish, and as we look further into their lives, His faithfulness is proven.

Reading on in 1 Samuel we learn what happened to Hannah, "It came about in due time, after Hannah had conceived, that she gave birth to a son; and she named him Samuel, *saying*, "because I have asked him of the LORD" (1 Samuel 1:20). So, we see that the Lord satisfied her longing for a child.

The Lord replenishes, to Job, his health and wealth as well as giving back his friends and giving him a new family, as follows:

> "…the LORD restored the fortunes of Job when he prayed for his friends, and the LORD increased all that Job had twofold. Then all his brothers and all his sisters and all who had known him before came to him, and they ate bread with him in his house; and they consoled him and comforted him for all the adversities that the LORD had brought on him. And each one gave him one piece of money and each a ring of gold. The LORD blessed the latter *days* of Job more than his beginning; and he had 14,000 sheep and 6,000 camels and 1,000 yoke of oxen and 1,000 female donkeys. He had seven sons and three daughters." (Job 42:10-13)

Finally, we look at David's life. He says, "I will extol thee, O LORD; for You have lifted me up, And have not let my enemies to rejoice over me" (Psalm 30:1). The Lord did not allow him to be overtaken by his enemies. 2 Samuel 22 tells of David's song after deliverance from the hand of all his enemies and from the hand of Saul. Psalm 18 uses the words of the song in 2 Samuel 22.

> "I call upon the LORD, who is worthy to be praised, And I am saved from my enemies …He brought me forth also into a broad place; He rescued me, because He delighted in me. The LORD has rewarded me according to my righteousness; According to the cleanness of my hands He has recompensed me." (Psalm 18:3, 19-20)

The Lord promises soul restoration and from these few examples we see Him doing just that, restoring the souls of men and women. Whether it is loss, infertility, enemy attack, or any number of difficulties, life on this earth causes distress. Our souls, our lives, need restoration from the pain that circumstances inflict on us.

The Lord desires for us to turn to Him with the situations that disturb us, with the conditions in which our souls are left. The Lord desires that we come to know Him. He wants us to know His character. The Lord's ultimate desire is that we come to know Him and His unconditional love for us as individuals.

Each scriptural example we just looked at show the Lord's deliverance, and solutions to the problems or replacement of those losses. Yet in other times, the soul is restored without the difficulty of the burden being lifted from us. In other words, we go through the trial and its effects on us. James 4:8 tells us to draw near to Him and He will draw near to us.

As we bring Him the conditions of our souls, He leads us to find deeper intimacy with Him. He draws us to lean on, to depend upon, and trust in Him for His outcome. His outcome may not be exactly what we think should happen or want to have happen. When we are willing to let go of the outcome, and can stop trying to manipulate circumstances to get our way, it is then that we come to find Him as our full satisfaction. We grow to know Him more as we seek relationship with Him in the midst of our circumstances, good or bad.

We can see evidence of the Lord's will for our dependence on Him as Paul goes to the Lord with the complaint of a "thorn in the flesh", a problem causing him limitations in serving the way he desires. Paul desires that this "thorn" be removed, but the Lord refuses to do so, instead He answers Paul, "My grace is sufficient for you, for power is perfected in weakness." (2 Corinthians 12:9).

Paul is asked to remain with the bothersome problem and to trust God for the sufficiency of His grace to live his life. The point being, we do not bring our conditions of soul to Him to make our lives easy, but rather for the purpose of restoration according to His will, that we might really know our Shepherd who alone satisfies the deepest core of our being—*the Shepherd who restores*. He wants us to know, that no matter what the circumstance is, He can restore the condition of our soul. The soul is restored in knowing the Restorer, not in the change or removal of the circumstance. We are perfected through the trial.

What comes to mind is an old wooden chair that was picked up at a rummage sale. To one person it may look like a piece of junk, but to another who can look at it with the realization of what it could be, it is a treasure. The rescued chair may be wobbly and covered with many coats of paint, yet with a little elbow grease it can become a masterpiece. Under the layers of paint, the person finds the beautiful wood grain and once the legs are made steady, it is restored for the work for which it was made. So it is with us, we must be pulled out of our sinfulness and made in newness, to be like Him. He takes all the broken, ugly parts, and by His Holy Spirit, works on us. Remember, we too were created for His purposes and the Lord knows what our potential is.

My Life Experience:
Personal Testimony

A number of years ago, I went through a debilitating depression. Intense counseling helped me to deal with my abandonment and replacement feelings. The counseling brought me to understand the emptiness in my heart and to realize there were issues I had stuffed deep inside. Working through those issues made my neediness seem greater, which was very painful. It seemed safer to me to seek my help from my counselor despite her effort to point me to the Lord instead of her. I was determined to manipulate the outcome in order to have my needs met my way. Therefore, rather than giving my need to God, I gave my neediness to the counselor. I wanted her to, somehow, fix the huge hole in my heart.

Even though I knew the Lord was with me, I felt alone. As a result, I became very dependent on the counselor to meet my emotional needs. It was around this time that the Lord began to lead me to the book of Jeremiah and through the Kay Arthur study of *"Lord Heal My Hurts."* It took me a long time to realize what I had been doing and what the Lord was putting His finger on in my life. The following verse spoke to my heart convicting me of sin, "For My people have committed two evils; They have forsaken me, The fountain of living waters, To hew for themselves cisterns, Broken cisterns That can hold no water." (Jeremiah 2:13). The Lord prompted me to turn to Him. I wasn't ready.

It took me a long time to realize how I too had forsaken the Lord and tried to find my own solutions. Finally, I realized my sin of idolatry in giving my neediness to the counselor, rather than seeking Christ. The Lord showed me clearly that He wanted to meet my needs, but I thought I knew what was best for me. I, stubborn like the Israelites, spent some time in the wilderness of disobedience and didn't get to the promised land of healing; I hadn't gone to the Great Physician with my needs. The Lord led me to see how I needed to give Him my pain, neediness and every desire of my heart. He wanted me to wait on Him, so He could meet me in my need with His own perfect way. At last, I realized that only the Lord had the power to heal me, He is the only True Source. The Lord doesn't waste any of our pain. Through this process, the Lord taught me compassion, a new willingness to love and to not hide from love out of fear. Although He has brought me from despair to joy in Him, He has left a certain degree of neediness in me. The neediness I am talking about is the longing for deep emotional connection, to not be invisible, to feel validated, to feel belonging, to want to touch others who are living with painful emotions due to emptiness, abandonment, and replacement. Just as Paul's thorn in the flesh helped him to find sufficiency in God's grace, I too see the sufficiency of God's grace in His perfect plan for my life, moment by moment and day by day. I have learned that I must be willing to go through pain and need, so honor, praise, love, and service to God can be birthed. The Lord has led me to know His purpose for my life, even His purpose in my pain and the balm of His healing love in the midst of it. He has shown me that when I am seeking help from anyone, if that person is not pointing me to the Lord, but instead rather allowing me to depend on him or her, I am heading for trouble.

My counselor, a Christian counselor, continually worked toward helping me to understand my need to walk according to what the Lord was leading me to understand. She helped me know the importance of depending on Him and the beauty of Him working through her to help me grow spiritually and emotionally, yet the Lord is the one who healed me. It took me a long time to turn my dependence fully upon the Lord.

The Lord's desire is for us to let Him be the Source that meets our needs in His perfect way (see Philippians 4:19). That means willingness to trust Him for the outcome He desires. For me that meant letting God really change me. Although trusting is very scary business for me, I have learned that His ways are always so much better than mine. He alone can feed my empty soul, and satisfy the deepest needs of my heart. The saying goes "hindsight is 20/20." I see now more clearly, how the Lord allowed my pain to draw me to Him. Although I knew Him, He knew that I failed in even beginning to understand the depth of His love for me and although I truly trusted Him for my salvation, I was still too afraid to trust Him with my raw pain and aching sense of neediness. I wanted to be in control, so I didn't have to feel. Yet, He wanted me to feel, so He could help me learn to know Him more intimately and allow His love to bring the much needed healing to my hurting heart.

He has satisfied my weary soul in amazing ways. He knew exactly what I needed in my life, so that He could use me to touch lives of others. One of the Psalmists expresses my feelings about the Lord's work in my life this way, "From *my* distress I called upon the LORD; The LORD answered me *and set me* in a large place" (Psalm 118:5). He freed me from my prison of pain. When we seek the Lord from whatever our "prison" may be, we can cry out with David, "Bring my soul out of prison, So that I may give thanks to Your name; The righteous will surround me, for You will deal bountifully with me" (Psalm 142:7).

A.M. Overton's poem describes God and His purposes vividly.

> My Father's way may twist and turn,
> My heart may throb and ache,
> But in my soul I'm glad I know,
> He maketh no mistake.

My cherished plans may go astray,
My hopes may fade away.
But still I'll trust my Lord to lead
For He doth know the way

Tho' night be dark and it may seem
That day will never break,
I'll pin my faith, my all in Him,
He maketh no mistake.

There's so much now I cannot see,
My eyesight's far too dim,
But come what may, I'll simply trust
And leave it all to Him.

For by and by the mist will lift
And plain it all he'll make.
Through all the way, tho' dark to me,
He made not one mistake.[6]

He is a God we can trust for soul restoration.

Reaching:
To Know Him More Through Prayer and Fasting

It is always the Lord's desire for us to know Him more. As I
travel through my journey of life, it becomes evident that in the
painful difficult times I am drawn to lean on Him and learn to
trust Him more deeply. In these times, I have learned more of His

---

[6] A.M. Overton. "Faith". Publisher unknown.

character, more of His attributes, and especially more of His love as He has touched me during my journey. But even when I am out of the valley, I have found that I need to seek to know Him more in His Word, and in ways He teaches. The Lord doesn't want any of us struggling through life on our own, blindly, without His strength and His wisdom. As I grow in the knowledge of Him and in my love of Him, I also see that He helps me to grow in Christ-likeness. He yearns for us to come away with Him and reach to know Him more.

One of the ways we can reach for Him is through prayer and fasting. Prayer and fasting are an important part of life as a Christian.

> …prayer needs fasting for its full and perfect development. Faith needs a life of prayer for its full growth. Faith can only live by feeding on what is Divine, on God himself.[7]

I find that I come to pray most often when I am feeling needy and helpless. Our neediness and helplessness is the cry of our soul, developing into the prayer of a soul in need of restoration. Remember *He restores my soul.* It is with that soul-need that we come, and reach out to Him in prayer. Where in your life do you find you are helpless? Pride and self-sufficiency often are roadblocks that have kept me from crying out to God with my

---

[7] Murray, Andrew. "With Christ in the School of Prayer". Public domain. http://www.ccel.org/ccel/murray.XIII.html

needs. I have come to realize that my seeking Him is not about getting a thing I desire, but that my heart fully desires Him alone, that my satisfaction might be found in Him. So, as I seek Him in prayer, I have learned that I will be most satisfied when He is my desire.

I express what prayer means to me in the following poem,

Prayer

Prayer is melting,

Melting in deep emotion at His feet

Full of despair and need

Overwhelmed and stressed

Doubting and fearful

Helpless and lonely

Bringing all of my neediness to Him

Pouring out my heart before Him

Words gushing out at times

Silent at other times

Joy and singing

Tears and sobbing

I come as I am

Bringing my needs, wants, desires and hopes

He takes it all

He takes my wounded self

He sees my true needs deeply beyond what I think or know

He speaks to my heart

He gently leads me to know His will

He transforms my heart

And in this transformation I become more like Him

I find that in His arms of love, His desires become mine
I want only to live for Him
I know His love yet wonder why or how
I stumble and trust
I walk and fall
He leads the way.
He guides me
He teaches me
He holds my soul
In all of life He shows me that in coming to Him
In pouring myself out to Him
He alone satisfies and gives abundant life.
He is always faithful no matter what I bring to Him.
In prayer I melt into a child running to daddy for all I need
I ask, Sweet Abba, restore me.
Sweet Abba waits with a loving heart to meet me
I am at home in His love.
He is all I need and more
In prayer—In Him I abide.

Abiding in Him is what the Lord calls us to do, to find all we need in Him. In abiding, we grasp onto the Father as a small child grasps their daddy's hand. We trust in His sovereignty and providence. My prayer is the cry of my soul put in words and my Heavenly Father responds. *He restores my soul.*

> Prayer is the one hand with which we grasp the invisible. Fasting is the other hand, the one with which we let go of the visible.[8]

When choosing to fast, we are to consider the state of our hearts. Just as a fast cleanses our bodies, prayer cleanses our hearts as the Lord works in us to confess, repent, and find healing. As our bodies become emptied in the fast, our hearts can be cleansed by prayer and filled with spiritual food as we deepen our relationship with the Lord, seeking to know Him and His will more completely.

We see that we are called to fast in Matthew 6:16 following the prayer model our Lord taught us. Jesus speaks of "when we fast" and tells us not to act as hypocrites in our fasts.

Fasting is "abstinence from anything that hinders our communion with God." . . . "Fasting intensifies our prayer, allowing us to reach into the innermost part of our spirit till we can understand spiritual things that we otherwise couldn't grasp." "Fasting helps us to find God's will."[9]

At this point, you may be asking yourself questions regarding how to go about fasting. The intent of this chapter is not to teach the how-to's of fasting, so for further information please check the

---

[8] Murray, Andrew. "With Christ in the School of Prayer ". Public domain. http://www.ccel.org.ccel/murray.XIII.html

[9] © 2004 Charles Stanley. Handle With Prayer published by David C. Cook. Publisher permission required to reproduce. All rights reserved.

Recommended Readings section at the back of the book. Here you will find books with the information that can help you fast in ways that benefit you and your walk with the Lord.

The Scriptures give us many excellent examples of fasting in both the Old and the New Testament. I chose just a few examples, which will help us in learning the purpose in fasting. As we learn these people's purposes, we too may find reason and purpose to fast. More examples of fasting can be found by doing a word study on fasting with the use of a good Bible concordance and your Bible.

- Ezra called for a fast as he was returning from Babylon because he needed protection and desired to know the right way to go. Ezra tells, "Then I proclaimed a fast there at the river of Ahava, that we might afflict ourselves before our God to seek him a safe journey for us, our little ones and all our possessions" (Ezra 8:21). He knew he could not provide the kind of protection that he and his men needed. He knew that the Lord could. He sought the Lord in his neediness, in his helplessness.

- In 2 Samuel 12:16a we find David fasting because of sin. His fast was in response to Nathan leading him to recognize the ugliness of his sin with Bathsheba when he had Uriah killed. He fasted in repentance and in prayer that their child would not die. The ultimate need of our soul is to have restored relationship with God. When that relationship is broken by sin, we might also pray that sin's consequences be removed. This is what David does. You can read the words of his repentant heart in Psalms 32 and 51.

- We often find the prophets fasting because of the sins of their people. Nehemiah says, "When I heard these words, I sat down and wept and mourned for days; and I was fasting and praying before the God of heaven" (Nehemiah 1:4). Nehemiah goes on in the succeeding verses with a prayer of repentance.

- The widow Anna chose to serve God by fasting and praying both night and day (Luke 2:38). Serving God with a humble heart, praying and fasting is something anyone can do. There are so many whose souls need restoration in knowing Jesus as Lord and Savior.

- Jesus gives us another purpose for fasting when He tells the disciples, in Matthew 17:15-26, that sometimes prayer and fasting are necessary to release people from demon possession.

Today many people are trapped in bondage to drugs, gambling, or other addictions. Any type of bondage is a reason for the need of prayer and fasting. Anytime we have a problem that we need the Lord's help in taking care of, we can seek Him with fervent hearts as we fast and pray for His intervention, and answers, in regard to whatever is going on in our lives.

In summary, some of the reasons for fasting we see in the Scriptures are for protection, for guidance and direction, in repentance, as an act of service, and for release from bondage including demon possession.

The Scriptures clearly state what the Lord desires and rejects in our fasting. In order to learn of this we go to Isaiah 58.

> "Yet they seek, inquire for, *and* require Me daily and delight [externally] to know My ways, as [if they were in reality] a nation that did righteousness and forsook not the ordinance of their God. They ask of Me righteous judgments, they delight to draw near to God [in visible ways], Why have we fasted, they say, and You do not see it? Why have we afflicted ourselves, and you take no knowledge [of it]? Behold [O Israel], on the day of your fast [when you should be grieving for your sins], you find profit in your business, and [instead of stopping all work, as the law implies you and your workmen should do] you extort from your hired servants a full amount of labor." Isaiah 58:2-3 (AMP)

The Israelites went through the motions of seeking God, but lived lives of disobedience. They did visible things to look good on the outside, but had filthy hearts. They were hypocrites. They sought profit in their business and expected their servants to work, so they could make money. This was appalling to the Lord, because the Israelites were still thinking about self and their hearts did not desire the Lord. Jesus says "Woe to you, scribes and Pharisees, hypocrites! For you clean the outside of the cup and of the dish, but inside they are full of robbery and self-indulgence" (Matthew 23:25).

The Israelites fasted and afflicted themselves but their hearts were hard and full of pride and their lives were full of self-indulgence. We just briefly read about Nehemiah. His fast was an example of an acceptable fast. He had a humble heart and he offered a prayer of repentance to his Holy Father God.

Fasting isn't supposed to be merely mechanical, just going through the motions to make us look good. When we come with a repentant heart and a humble spirit, emptied of self, we can better concentrate on the filling and feeding of our souls. The Lord seeks to convict the hearts of His people as He asks,

> "Is such a fast as yours what I have chosen, a day for a man to humble himself with sorrow in his soul? [Is true fasting merely mechanical?] Is it only to bow down his head like a bulrush and to spread sackcloth and ashes under him [to indicate a condition

of heart that he does not have]? Will you call this a fast, and an acceptable day to the Lord?" Isaiah 58: 5 (AMP)

The Israelites didn't understand why it wasn't always honoring to God when they fasted.

Our hearts are readied for fasting by emptying ourselves of our sinful attitudes, to have a true humble heart of repentance. To get a true picture of this you may want to read Nehemiah's prayer in Nehemiah chapter one.

Fasting according to the Lord's choosing is to: "…loose the bonds of wickedness, to undo the bands of the yoke, to let the oppressed go free and that you break every [enslaving] yoke" (Isaiah 58:6). Wickedness is sin that places anything before or above God in our lives. The Israelites were putting their work and desires before truly worshiping the Lord. They were enslaved. Things and duties kept them apart from relationship with Him. Do you find yourself bound with any enslaving yokes, things that keep you apart from relationship with the Lord? Is it a television program that you can't miss? Addictions? The mall? A piece of technology? He wants us to break those enslaving yokes. He wants us to seek Him and His will, first (Matthew 6:33). Fasting according to the Lord's choosing is to: "…divide your bread with the hungry and bring the homeless poor into your house— when you see the naked, that you cover him, and that you hide not yourself from [the needs of] your own flesh and blood." Isaiah

58:7 (AMP). These words make it clear that fasting isn't about selfishness, but rather about selflessness. He wants us to Himself, emptying ourselves to receive from Him so we can give. He wants us to take what we have and give it or share it. He doesn't want us to hide ourselves away from the needy, hungry, homeless, poor, or naked. In denying self, we imitate Christ, who gave everything in order to serve us. Romans 12:1KJV says "I beseech you therefore, brethren, by the mercies of God, that ye present your bodies a living sacrifice, holy, acceptable unto God, which is your reasonable service."

When I come before God and sit in His presence, I find myself overwhelmed by the great magnitude of His love and mercy that He has bestowed upon me. In this, I have come to understand that sacrificial living comes out of knowing His love and mercy, as I look upon Him. I know how His love has *restored my soul* and continues to restore me daily, and knowing that makes me want to live it out.

How does great love and mercy get fleshed out in the here and now, in your life and mine? Based on the fast in Isaiah 58, the fast that the Lord called the Israelites to, ask yourself how or what you can sacrifice for another. Will I give a place to the homeless to live? Will I pay the bill that goes unpaid for the jobless one? Will I send money to the needy missionary? Will I use my time for me or for the furthering of the kingdom?

Too often, I find myself taking the way of comfort and pleasure rather than the way of sacrifice. It is His work, in us, that leads us to live out His love in giving and serving. My heart is too hard and unyielding when I am all consumed with busyness. Thinking about this leads me to realize even more the importance of setting aside time to pray and fast.

Isaiah goes on to explain how the Lord promises to honor those that come to Him in humility, in a spirit of repentance, in selflessness, in willingness to serve and to give.

> "Then shall your light break forth like the morning and your healing (your restoration and the power of a new life) shall spring forth speedily; your righteousness (your rightness, your justice, and your right relationship with God) shall go before you [conducting you to peace and prosperity], and the glory of the Lord shall be your rear guard. [Exodus 14:19, 20; Isa.51:12.] Then you shall call, and the Lord will answer; you shall cry and He will say, Here I am. If you take away from your midst yokes of oppression, [wherever you find them], the finger pointed in scorn and every form of false, harsh, unjust and wicked speaking, [Exod. 3:14.] And if you pour out that with which you sustain your own life for the hungry and satisfy the need of the afflicted, then shall your light rise in darkness, and your obscurity *and* gloom become like the noonday. And the Lord shall guide you continually and satisfy you in drought *and* in dry places and make strong your bones. And you shall be like a watered garden and like a spring of water, whose waters fail not." Isaiah 58:8-11 (AMP)

Here he promises "restoration." He promises "new life." *He restores my soul.*

Although the world pressures us to be independent and self-sufficient, God desires for us to depend on Him. He desires for us to live to delight in Him that He might feed us with His faithfulness, because it is in knowing His faithfulness we learn to know Him as our Shepherd. He desires to show us all He can do, just as the truths of His Word promise. We can fully put our trust in Him, because of our knowing He is sovereign, that He never fails us and He never forsakes us. We can pour out our hearts, full of desperation, anxiety, and need, fully trusting Him to care for us, fully trusting Him to restore our soul. We are encouraged to "Trust in him at all times; ye people, pour out your heart before him; God is a refuge for us. Selah" Psalm 62:8 (KJV).

Our neediness is only answered in His sufficiency, fasting brings the blessing of being filled with the Lord and of growing in deeper intimacy with Him. Prayer and fasting are disciplines of the heart that demonstrate devotion to God and reliance on God to fully satisfy us in all things. In prayer and fasting *our souls are restored.*

Questions:
For Life Application

1. Consider your life; when in your life have you known the soul restoration power of the Lord? How is your hope increased by knowing His soul restoration power?

2. How has He used your pain? Has your pain drawn you into deeper intimacy with the Lord? How is this evident in your life? Whose life can you touch and encourage by sharing the Lord's work in your life?

3. Consider: Who is God to you? Tell Him, "Lord, You
    are…., I believe [this about You] and because I believe
    [this about You] I [can or can't] trust You with my heart."

4. What sins are holding you hostage? Who are you keeping
    in bondage? Who can you free with forgiveness, showing
    them the grace that the Lord has shown to you?

5. Ask the Lord to open your eyes to the state of your heart.

    Psalm 139:23-24 KJV says:

    "Search me, O God, and know my heart: try me and know my thoughts: And see if *there be any* wicked way in me, and lead me in the way everlasting." Write in your journal or on a piece of paper the thoughts that come to mind as you ask the Lord to look into your heart.

Chapter 3

His Leading in Paths of Righteousness

Psalm 23:3b (ESV) "...He leads me in paths of righteousness for his name's sake."

He is My Shepherd to Lead and to Guide

This Shepherd who brings us to satisfaction and restoration in our souls is also the Shepherd who leads (ESV) and guides (NASB) us. The Scriptures say,

> "[Live] as children of obedience [to God]; do not conform yourselves to the evil desires [that governed you] in your former ignorance [when you did not know the requirements of the Gospel]. But as the One Who called you is holy, you yourselves also be holy in all your conduct and manner of living. For it is written, You shall be holy, for I am holy." 1 Peter 1:14-16 (AMP)

The Lord desires for us to walk according to His will, in the paths of justice and holiness. He desires for us to walk in integrity. David cried out to God to be led and to be taught so that he would know how to walk in the paths of righteousness. He said to the Lord, "Lead me in Your truth and teach me, for You are the God of my salvation; for You I wait all the day" (Psalm 25:5) and "Teach me thy way, O LORD, and lead me in a plain path, because of mine enemies" (Psalm 27:11 (KJV)).

Our Shepherd Christ leads and guides us for His name's sake. The path we walk should bring glory to His name. We are called to obedience and to self-control in our spiritual and moral behavior in every area and relationship of our lives. As we begin to take a look at the area of obedience, we will learn about temptation and how to triumph over sin.

Digging Deeper and Defining:
The Process of Temptation

We live in a world filled with temptations. All you have to do is turn on the television, see a movie, go to the mall, look at a newspaper, a magazine, a billboard or visit a friend and you are bombarded with temptations. Sometimes being tempted doesn't even require getting out of bed; it just starts with a thought.

James 1:14-15 says, "But each one is tempted when he is

carried away and enticed by his own lust. Then when lust has conceived, it gives birth to sin; and when sin is accomplished, it brings forth death."

We are tempted when something looks inviting or is attractive to us, increasing our desire for it. Temptation leads us away from God toward someone or something that we want. Following attractions and desires can draw us into the wrong relationships, actions, or places leading us into sin.

The Lord's Word/The Lord's Work: Triumph over Sin; Choosing Obedience

We see temptation leading to sin illustrated numerous times in the Bible. Let's look at a few examples:

- In 2 Samuel 11 and 12 we find David relaxing out on the porch, because he had chosen to not go with his men to war. While he was out there "he saw a woman bathing; and the woman was very beautiful in appearance" (2 Samuel 11: 2). Bathsheba is bathing, David looks and is enticed by her beauty. David decides he wants her and makes the first step in getting what he wants, by inquiring about her. The end of Verse three tells us, "And one said, Is not this

Bathsheba, the daughter of Eliam, the wife of Uriah, the Hittite" (2 Samuel 11:3)? Someone reminds David who she is and whose she is. Here is the way out, but David misses it; he ignores that person and sends messengers to get her. She comes in by him and he lies with her.

1 Corinthians 10:13 (AMP) says:

> "For no temptation (no trial regarded as enticing to sin), [no matter how it comes or where it leads] has overtaken you *and* laid hold on you that is not common to man [that is, no temptation or trial has come to you that is beyond human resistance and that is not adjusted and adapted and belonging to human experience, and such as man can bear]. But God is faithful [to His Word and to His compassionate nature], and He [can be trusted to] not to let you be tempted *and* tried *and* assayed beyond your ability *and* strength of resistance *and* power to endure, but with the temptation He will [always] also provide the way out (the means of escape to a landing place), that you may be capable *and* strong and powerful to bear up under it patiently."

We see even more sin conceived as David plots to cover up his sin by calling Uriah home so he will lie with his wife, but Uriah refuses and David puts him in the front lines of battle so that he is killed. How easily we become blinded to the right thing to do when the wrong thing is so inviting. Later in 2 Samuel we see that Bathsheba conceives and in chapter 12 we find the consequence of sin. The child dies.

- Another example is that of Ananias and Sapphira in Acts 5. It seemed like such a good thing to do, to sell the land and then even better to give the proceeds to the church, but one problem, greed, and selfishness get in the way. So, they only give part of the money and then boldly lie about it. Peter shows them their sin, and Ananias tells a deliberate lie to try to deceive Peter. Peter says, "While it remained *unsold*, did it not remain your own? And after it was sold, was it not under your control? Why is it that you have conceived this deed in your heart? You have not lied to men but to God." (Acts 5:4)

  Though Satan filled his heart to do it, yet he is said to have conceived it in his own heart, which shows that we cannot extenuate our sins by laying the fault of them upon the devil; he tempts, but he cannot force; it is of our own lusts that we are drawn away and enticed. The evil thing, whatever it is, that is said or done, the sinner has conceived it in his own heart. [10]

When Sapphira is asked about the incident she gives a similar answer seemingly not even knowing that her husband is dead. Ananias and his wife Sapphira both die immediately after responding to Peter with lies. We are so easily enticed even though

---

[10] Gills, John. John Gills Exposition of the Bible is in the public domain and may be freely used and distributed. http://www.biblestudytools.com/commentaries/gills-exposition-of-the-bible/act-5/

we are told:

> "For all that is in the world – the lust of the flesh [craving for
> sensual gratification] and the lust of the eyes [greedy longings of
> the mind} and the pride of life [assurance in one's own
> resources or in the stability of earthly things]– these do not
> come from the Father but are from the world [itself]. And the
> world passes away *and* disappears and with it the forbidden
> cravings (the passionate desires, the lust) of it; but he who does
> the will of God and carries out His purposes in his life abides
> (remains) forever." 1 John 2:16-17 (AMP)

Satan goes to great lengths to entice. We learn in Luke 4:1-13
that Satan also tempted Jesus. These verses illustrate for us times
of vulnerability to temptation that are applicable for our lives.
First, we see that Satan tempts us when we are weak and urges us
to take what we desire or think would give us what we need. Jesus
was hungry and Satan tells Him to prove Himself as the Son of
God by commanding the stones to be made into bread. Satan
wants us to find sustenance in anything but God and His Word.
Jesus answered him, "It is written, 'MAN SHALL NOT LIVE ON
BREAD ALONE' " (Luke 4:4). Then we see that Satan offers what is
not his to give, he offers a phony or a substitute in order to receive
worship. Satan lies to Jesus, seeking glory for himself, when he
says, "And he led Him up and showed Him all the kingdoms of
the world in a moment of time. And the devil said to Him, "`I will
give You all this domain and its glory; for it has been handed over

to me, and I give it to whomever I wish. Therefore if You worship before me, it shall all be Yours' " (Luke 4:5-7). The kingdoms of the world are not Satan's to give. Satan wants us to accept his lies over truth, especially over the truth of the Word. Satan easily and subtly blinds and deceives us. He leads people down paths that make them think they are good and acting right until they no longer care as long as they get what they want. He leads them into traps of religion and traditions, into idolatry, self-sufficiency, and selfishness. But, the Lord *"leads me in paths of righteousness for His name's sake."*

What is the take away value from all of this? It is important that I constantly guard my heart and seek to know God more because when I am not seeking to do this, Satan sneaks in, in my attitudes and responses, in my mind and then into my behavior and the way I live. Proverbs 4:23 (NIV) says, "Above all else, guard your heart, for it is the wellspring of life."

It is so easy to be lured into one of Satan's traps. It is so easy to get hooked by temptation in this world and pulled into sin as we are tempted. How are you tempted? What lures you? I know there are specific areas in my life where I can easily be pulled into sin. I get hooked into believing that things can satisfy me and that somehow my needs can be met apart from God. This is what the discontentment was about that I spoke of in chapter 1, My Life Experience, "Wandering Like a Sheep." I begin to think that things can fill the emptiness inside or that people will like me better, or accept me more if I please them. However, I soon learn how much these lack in satisfying me. So, what can we do to steer clear from the path of sin?

We can again look to the Scriptures to find examples of how to triumph over sin. We start out with David, who because of his success in life has antagonized Saul to the point of desiring to kill him. At one time Saul goes into a cave where David and his men already are and Saul is unaware of their presence. The men that are with David tell him that they will deliver Saul into his hands. How easy it would be for David to kill Saul and be rid of the constant worry of being stalked. David has the perfect opportunity. But, instead David cuts off a piece of Saul's skirt and forbids the men to harm him. He realizes the opportunity for sin, of which David's men have reminded him, and David stops the conceived act. Saul notices David's right choice and Saul is grateful (see 1 Samuel 24:1-22, 26:1-25).

We find another example of triumph over sin as we look into the life of Joseph (see Genesis 39). Joseph is in the house with Potiphar's wife who is attracted to him. Potiphar's wife pushes Joseph to lie with her, but rather than giving into her, he runs from her. We too need to run from sin. Lust is stopped, because he refuses and in fact, he leaves his garment in her hand as he quickly goes out of the room. His choice to leave the temptation is the way that brings Joseph triumph over what could have been a great sin. John 14:21 says, "He who has My commandments and keeps them is the one who loves Me; and he who loves Me will be loved by My Father, and I will love him and will disclose Myself to him." Our obedience demonstrates our love to the Lord.

It is our choice to obey or disobey God. He wants our submission to His will. The Lord is so good to offer us His wisdom, guidance and direction, yet we, like the Israelites, often choose our own ways. He gives us a promise to help us with the burden of obedience. He knows that we can't do life on our own. He knows how much we need Him in order to live the life we are called to live. He is present to *guide us in paths of righteousness*.

Matthew 11:28-30 says, "Come to Me, all who are weary and heavy-laden, and I will give you rest. Take My yoke upon you and learn from Me, for I am gentle and humble in heart, and YOU WILL FIND REST FOR YOUR SOULS. For My yoke is easy and My burden is light."

The yoke according to the ATS Bible Dictionary is "a symbol of subjection and servitude."[11] When we think of the purpose of the yoke, it was to make the burden lighter. The yoke was used to help the young untrained ox learn from the older ox that led it.

To choose to take on the Rabbi's yoke means you will trust him because you believe His teachings are completely right. There is no picking and choosing allowed. Just as the oxen were yoked together, we, too, need to take the yoke of Jesus.

---

[11] Rand, W.W. "Entry for YOKE", "American Tract Society Bible Dictionary" http://www.studylight.org/dic/ats/view.cgi?number=T2228. 1859 Public domain.

> "My yoke" here means "the service of God as I teach it'…
> and the emphasis is on "my." The contrast is not between
> "yoke" and "no yoke" but between "my teaching" (light yoke)
> and "the current scribal teaching; (heavy yoke)."[12]

We need to accept His teaching as the truth that it is and be in submission to Him. We demonstrate an attitude of submission by walking in obedience and living a life of service to Him. Today, we still have a choice to live life laboring and heavy-laden or to put on His yoke and serve Him and find rest. In Him, we find guidance in *the paths of righteousness*, yet so often, we choose to fight against Him in disobedience.

The Pharisees had a different view of obedience:

> "Then Jesus spoke to the crowds and to His disciples, saying;
> "The scribes and the Pharisees have seated themselves in the
> chair of Moses; therefore all that they tell you, do and observe,
> but do not do according to their deeds; for they say *things* and do
> not do *them*. They tie up heavy burdens and lay them on men's
> shoulders, but they themselves are unwilling to move them with
> so *much* as a finger. But they do all their deeds to be noticed by
> men; for they broaden their phylacteries and lengthen the tassels
> of their garments." (Matthew 23:1-5)

---

[12]Orr, James, M.A. ,D. D. General Editor, "Entry for 'YOKE'". "International Standard Bible Encyclopedia".< http://www.studylight.org/enc/isb/view.cgl?number=T9259>. 1915 **Public Domain.**

The phylactery was a leather box, cube-shaped, closed with an attached flap and bound to the person by a leather band.[13]

The tassels referred to here are those explained in Numbers 15:37-40:

> The LORD also spoke to Moses, saying, 'Speak to the sons of Israel, and tell them that they shall make for themselves tassels on the corners of their garments throughout their generations, and that they shall put on *the tassel of each corner a cord of blue.* It shall be a tassel for you to look at and remember all the commandments of the LORD, so as to do them and not follow after your own heart and your own eyes, after which you played the harlot, so that you may remember to do all My commandments and be holy to your God.' (emphasis mine).

The teachings of the Pharisees and those of Jesus are as different as night and day. The Pharisees taught the law with added rules and regulations, which actually blinded people to the heart of the Law. They emphasized behavior, with guilt as its motivation. The teaching of Jesus is inward (touching the heart of the Law) and can only be accomplished by the Holy Spirit – a transformation motivated by His love. His love for us is always for the purpose of bringing us closer to Him, to lead us to be a Holy people, and to lead us to bring glory to His name. It is the perfect plan of this love that sent Jesus to die for us and give us eternal

---

[13] Orr, James, M.A., D.D. General Editor, "Entry for 'PHYLACTERY'". "International Standard Bible Encyclopedia". http://www.studylight.org/enc/isb/view.cgi?number=T6920. 1915. Public Domain.

life. How can we doubt this love? In order for us to walk in the Lord's will and live a life of obedience we need to seek His wisdom in prayer. As we grow in our heart knowledge of Him, our willingness to trust and obey becomes more evident. We desire and learn to walk in His *paths of righteousness* because of His guidance through relationship with our Shepherd.

So, we have seen how we are so easily pulled into sin's traps and led astray. The Bible gives us truths to guide us in the paths of righteousness, to help us learn to live in victory. Proverbs 12:12b (KJV) says, "the root of the righteous yieldeth fruit."

When we are rooted in Jesus (Ephesians 3:14-21) and know Him as the root of our righteousness with the indwelling of the Holy Spirit, it is then that we can walk by the Spirit, and yield His fruit. What grows out of my life, my fruit or lack of it, makes known to those around me a picture of my root. I need to consider daily what my fruit looks like. Am I growing in righteousness and yielding fruit that brings glory to the Lord? *He guides me in the paths of righteousness for His name's sake.* As we are satisfied and nourished in God's law, meditating on His Word, and feeding on His faithfulness, we see His will as our food and we grow to bear fruit.

Isaiah 48:17 says: "Thus says the LORD, your Redeemer, the Holy One of Israel, I am the Lord, your God, who teaches you to profit, *Who leads you in the way you should go*" (emphasis mine).

My Life Experience:
Waiting for God's Leading

It is very easy for us humans to walk according to our own agendas and end up going ahead of the Lord. One lesson I learned the hard way is the importance of waiting for the Lord to keep me in step with Him and not off on my own path. I had felt the Lord's leading following my depression to do topical retreats at my church for small groups of women. I began to do these quarterly. The Lord had been very specific in showing me what He wanted me to do. Initially, I was very hesitant and unsure about this. It was a stretch for me; it took me out of my comfort zone. I didn't like leading and I was afraid of speaking in front of a group. But, as my confidence grew in Him, I did move forward with enthusiasm and the Lord was gracious in giving me the teachings. I started out using materials of others, but gradually I found how the Lord was using my quiet times with Him as a resource. He taught me what I needed to know and gave me the wisdom to know how to share it effectively. He blessed my retreats and I grew in confidence, not necessarily a good thing. I began to really enjoy doing the retreats and started to feel as though there must be more that I could do.

In my attempt to do even more, to try to act on my desire to please the Lord more, I jumped into a leadership position in women's ministry. This was not my calling and was outside of the

Lord's leading. Rather, I thought this was something I could do.
Once again, I wasn't depending upon the Lord. I was thinking of
what I could do. In my own mind, I saw many possibilities, but
even with great effort and much help from others, nothing took
off. This made me think of the Israelites when Joshua, Caleb and
others, had gone to spy out the land the Israelites, gave in to fear.
However, after they realized their sin against the Lord, they
decided to go anyway, even though Moses warned. Moses told
them, "Do not go up, or you will be struck down before your
enemies, for the LORD is not among you" (Numbers 14:42). I had
chosen a path separate from His most perfect will. I was going in
my own strength, for my own glory. After about a year, the Lord
led me to see that this had never been His will for me in the first
place. In other words, I took what He gave me to do and went
further than what I should have. He had clearly directed me to do
the retreats but nothing more. He had clearly blessed the retreats. I
did not have the leadership ability or qualities for a ministry
leadership position. I did not have the women of the church
behind me, because I was a behind-the-scenes type person and not
well-known. It had been my own will, not the Lord's. This all had
come out of my own thinking and my own desire. After I realized
what I had done, I gave up the position; however, I learned some
very important lessons. I needed to follow the Lord's direction and
walk in obedience to Him. I needed to be totally dependent on
Him. I needed to take time to pray about each decision. As well as

all of this is, I recognized the hidden snare of pride in me and how important humility is in being God's servant.

The following is the poem I wrote from my experience:

From the Ash Heap

Many possibilities,
Opportunities galore.
His will was clear
But I wanted more.

Wanting to serve Him,
So wholeheartedly,
My overzealous desire,
Got the best of me.

Thinking more was better,
I reached for it all.
After all I could do it
Yet my will, not His call.

So, I took it all on
And it turned into sand
I have accomplished nothing
He fulfilled that which He planned.

Now, I'm filled with regret.
Realizing that I was wrong,
I didn't wait for His timing,
I chose my own song.

He had given me His plan,
I was to listen and obey.
It was what He desired,
I see that clearly today.

So, now I sit in the ash-heap,
There's nothing that I did gain,
Except the lessons I learned,
From the great endured pain.

I can choose to live my way,
Or I can listen fully to Him.
He fulfills His will only,
What's not for His glory is sin.

I have learned in my mistake,
That in my desires I can't trust.
Only His plan satisfies my heart,
I am His vessel made of dust.

It is obvious I started off on the right track, depending on the
Lord for His wisdom and leading, but soon my prideful thoughts
led me off into the track of my own will. I was no longer choosing

to harness my desires and goals by seeking to fulfill the Lord's plan. It suddenly became all about me and what I could do.

Reaching:
To Take Every Thought Captive

Our minds have a lot of power in our lives. Proverbs 23:7 (KJV) says, "For as a man thinketh in his heart so is he . . . " So much of our problem with self-control begins with what we do with the thoughts that pop into our minds.

The apostle Paul shares, ". . . but I see a different law in the members of my body, waging war against the law of my mind and making me a prisoner of the law of sin which is in my members" (Romans 7:23). He goes on to speak of the outcome of this war in how it plays out in our relationships to God. He explains it this way:

> "For those who are according to the flesh set their minds on the things of the flesh, but those who are according to the Spirit, the things of the Spirit. For the mind set on the flesh is death, but the mind set on the Spirit is life and peace, because the mind set on the flesh is hostile toward God; for it does not subject itself to the law of God, for it is not even able *to do so*, and those who are in the flesh cannot please God." (Romans 8:5-8)

These verses clearly show us the havoc sin plays in our lives. My lack of obedience in waiting for the Lord's leading in my ministry clearly demonstrates a lack of self-control.

One morning during devotional time with the Lord, He impressed on me what self-control really is. Self-control is putting me in a box and letting the Spirit work through me. When I am self-controlled, I am Spirit-yielded. So, I have learned I must continually ask myself, whom am I putting in the box? Is it God or me? I put God in the box, shutting myself off from hearing Him, when I allow myself to listen to and believe the lies of Satan. The Enemy has one goal and that is to cause us to doubt the goodness of God. For example, the Lord had given me the opportunity to do the retreats, but rather than being satisfied with that alone I thought, *there must be more I can do.* And, although it may look good and seemed like it would please God, it was pride and disobedience not to do only what He wanted me to do. Satan leads us to think we can do, have, or need more than what God has given us. Satan wants to weaken and destroy us by drawing us away from God and His will. Scripture tells us that our minds need to be renewed. Romans 12:2 says, "And do not be conformed to this world, but be transformed by the renewing of your mind, so that you may prove what the will of God is, that which is good and acceptable and perfect."

To not be conformed to the world takes self-control, to be transformed means we must yield self to the Holy Spirit.

Temptation is all around. We see something, and desire it and too often go after it to fill the emptiness inside of us. That is why we have closets stuffed to overflowing, and keys for buildings for extra storage, yet we still think that we need more or want more. The only real way to glorify the Lord Jesus Christ is to think according to His Word, and let the Spirit work through the Word to transform our hearts, *to guide us in the paths of righteousness*. We believe so many lies from Satan; we just receive, accept, and believe them. There are lies about our worth, our rights, our sin, our body, our desires, our needs, our relationships and many, many more. We can defeat Satan and the lies he tries to destroy us with by seeking the truth of the Word. Some verses that have helped me in this area are:

> "…greater is He who is in you than he who is in the world." (1 John 4:4b)

> "We are destroying speculations and every lofty thing raised up against the knowledge of God, and *we are* taking every thought captive to the obedience of Christ." (2 Corinthians 10:5)

> "…you will know the truth, and the truth shall make you free." (John 8:32)

Telling ourselves the Truth, letting go of lies and replacing them with God's Truth brings us great freedom, leading us in the path of His will. There is power in His name, in His Word, and in yielding to the Holy Spirit in times of difficulty because of negative thoughts or feelings. Find His Truths to memorize and find freedom. Let's reach to take every thought captive, this is the first step in self-control in the life of the Christian. In the Appendix at back of this book I share some Truths of the Word that have helped me in defeating some of the lies of Satan.

David says, "*He leads me in paths of righteousness for His name's sake.*" So often, we are enticed and pulled into temptation. We miss the Lord's guidance in paths of righteousness, and end up walking in disobedience. Often our lack of self-control, our failure to put self in a box and to be Spirit-led, leads us to walk in disobedience. We end up following the wrong path, our thoughts held captive by Satan's lies. God's Word, His Truth, leads us in the *paths of righteousness.* The paths He guides us on result in glory and honor being given to His name, "For His name's sake." Which path will you choose? It is a moment-by-moment, day-by-day choice.

Questions:
For Life Application:

1. What is worth more to you than what you have or can have with the Lord?

2. How do you get hooked by cultural messages?

3. What lies does Satan use to lead you away?

4. Where does the emptiness come from when you are so easily drawn away and enticed?

5. Have you looked in the back of this book at some of Satan's lies and the truths of the Lord that can strengthen you against them?

6. What triumphs can you share? When have you turned away from sin?

7. How have you gotten ahead of the Lord and His leading in your life or in your ministry?

Enrich your life… your soul; take some time to read Andrew Murray's book, *Waiting on God*. Share your insights with someone.

Chapter 4

His Comfort in the Valley

Psalm 23:4 (ESV) "Even though I walk through the valley of the shadow of death, I will fear no evil, for you are with me; your rod and your staff, they comfort me."

My Life Experience:
The Comfort of His Presence

It was 12:20 A.M. I awoke from a sound sleep, startled. Immediately my heart and mind were filled with intense fear, not only the fears of being awaken, but the fears of the world jumped at me also. I lay in my bed grappling with thoughts of various horrible things that could happen, all of the "what-if's" attacked my mind. I thought back to the event of the Minnesota bridge collapse in which some people were injured and others died. I thought about the persecuted in other nations. I went on to think about the many diseases that can attack one's body and I began to experience terror within. I wondered, *"where do you find comfort?"* Oh, I knew the right answer, I knew deep down that comfort is found in the Lord; I knew that from experience, but somehow, it escaped me at that moment, as it had at other times. I wanted a quick fix knowing that none of the "what-if's" would occur. But, there are no guarantees in this life, at least, not in regard to health, accidents, or violence—you just never know what is going to happen.

As the saying goes, "life is fragile." I know that part well. The fragility of life, the lack of control of our own circumstances, and the vast amount of suffering around us, all added to the intensity of the fear within. I knew that there would be no returning to a restful sleep at least not at that moment. My mind was racing. I got out of bed and went into the living room, grabbed my Bible, my prayer journal, and sat down in my favorite chair. I began writing my fears to the Lord and found verses in His Word to reassure my heart that was brimming over with panic. Somehow, I realized, I was holding onto the fear within me, clutching it tightly and trying also to grasp comfort, but there was no room in my fist—no room in my heart. I continued to try to find the remedy for the anxiety and worry. Where was comfort? I said, "Lord, there are so many terrible things that happen in this world." I wondered how I could rest, how I could find peace, how could I relax with all of these horrific happenings flashing through my mind? I was reading the Bible verses that told me not to fear; but I remained fearful. I wanted a promise that would release me from my terror. What could I do to find comfort? Then suddenly it happened, I heard it clearly in my heart, it startled me, the words were, "BUT I AM HERE." That was it, four simple words and suddenly I knew it, I knew where comfort could be found. The comfort I searched for is found in His presence. Peace settled into my heart. Yes, Lord, you *are* here. You are my comfort. I suddenly experienced His presence. And in knowing that my Sweet Abba, the Creator God of the Universe, my Savior, and Deliverer was there with me, I no longer felt the fear as it emptied itself. In its place, the Comforter filled me with His peace. Amazing, and yet the words describing this event do not do it justice. His presence and the comfort He brings are not easily explained.

Digging Deeper and Defining: Walking through the Valley

David says: "*Even though I walk through the valley of the shadow of death, I will fear no evil for you are with me; your rod and your staff they comfort me.*" When you are walking through the valley of the shadow of death, the light is blocked, the place is dark and deep and it seems to be very hopeless. When I think of this part of the 23rd Psalm, it often makes me think of Job who lost family and belongings, as well as his own personal health. Still he said, "Though he slay me, yet will I trust him…" (Job 13:15 (KJV)).

Darkness can be a place of fear, yet David says he doesn't fear evil, he doesn't fear what Satan can do to him. He doesn't fear because he knows the protection and guidance offered by the Shepherd's rod and staff. David is saying:

> " though, I as one of the flock, should walk through the most dismal valley, in the dead of the night, exposed to pitfalls, precipices, devouring beasts, I should fear no evil under the guidance and protection of such a Shepherd. He knows all the passes, dangerous defiles, hidden pits and abrupt precipices in the way and He will guide me around, about and through them."[14]

David knows the Lord his Shepherd had often delivered him from dangerous situations. David knows the comfort of the Lord's presence in the valleys of life and he wasn't paralyzed there in the valley, but walks through. Evil lurks in the shadows and impending death is very real to the sheep. Yet David knows the Shepherd is present to protect him from danger and guide him to safety, so he has no need to fear the evil about.

What is it that blocks God's light for you, leaving you in the

---

[14] Clarke, Adam, "Commentary on Psalm 23". "The Adam Clarke Commentary". http://www.studylight.org/com/acc/view.cgi?book-ps&chapter=23 >. 1832. Public Domain.

shadow of death—a dark, deep, hopeless place?

I am writing this in a difficult time in my own personal life. At a time when the abandonment I am living in can feel like a dark, deep, hopeless place. The aloneness can leave me in a fearful state worrying about my own personal safety. And the brokenness of a relationship can feel like death. How can I know the comfort that David talks about?

David's comfort is in knowing the guidance and protection of his Shepherd. To know comfort in the valley of the shadow of death, I must trust in His presence with me. I must trust that He will guide and protect me. My fears either grow or diminish in relation to the level of my trust. As my fears grow, my hope disappears. My fear is directly related to my understanding of my ability to control a situation or circumstance. Fear is more and more present when the Shepherd's presence is less and less real to me. In my knowing the Lord's presence I can find rest. I can find comfort in the valley of the shadow of death. My fear dissipates like the clouds in the light of His presence.

The Lord's Word/The Lord's Work:
I AM

"BUT I AM HERE." These are the words His Spirit impressed upon my heart when my heart was so filled with fear. The word "but" is defined in the dictionary as "introducing contrast." Yes, it was as if He was saying you are fearful alone, however *I am* with you. *My* presence makes all the difference. The word "here" means "in this place"; right there with me. How much even those simple definitions add to the reality of the statement. And then I realized there was so much more meaning in the other two words. The words "I AM" are amazing words.

In Exodus, God has asked Moses to go to Pharaoh that he might bring forth the Israelites out of Egypt. The Lord promises to be with him.

> "And Moses said to God, Behold, when I come to the Israelites and say to them. The God of your fathers has sent me to you, and they say to me, What is His name? What shall I say to them? And God said to Moses, I AM WHO I AM *and* WHAT I AM I *and* WILL BE WHAT I WILL BE; and He said, you shall say this to the Israelites. I AM has sent me to you. God said also to Moses, This shall you say to the Israelites. The Lord, the God of your father, of Abraham, of Isaac, and of Jacob, has sent me to you! This is My name forever, and by this name I am to be remembered to all generations." (Exodus 3:13-15AMP)

God promises to be with Moses and refers to Himself as "I AM".
Moses felt fearful about going before Pharaoh and the LORD
promises His presence was to bring him comfort. Jesus also
reveals Himself with "I AM" statements in the New Testament.
The following seven statements help us to know more of Who He
is. Jesus was making it clear to the Jews to know His relationship
to the Father. The root meaning of Jehovah and LORD is I AM.
Jesus used the following "I am" titles in proving His deity. These
seven statements occur in the book of John.

1, "I am the bread of life . . . " John 6:35
2. "I am the Light of the world…" John 8:12
3. "I am the door . . . " John 10:9
4. "I am the good shepherd . . . " John 10:11
5. "I am the resurrection and the life . . . " John 11:25
6. "I am the way, the truth and the life . . . " John 14:6
7. "I am the true vine…" John 15:1

Let's take a closer look at each of these statements in light of
the comfort we can find in knowing the Lord and His presence.

- *John 6:35 "I am the bread of life . . . "*

The sufficiency of Jesus is summed up in the theme of bread.

Just as bread satisfies our physical hunger, Jesus is the Bread that satisfies our spiritual hunger. In Genesis, we are told that we will toil to make bread because of the curse God put on the ground, until we die and in death we will hopelessly return to dust –see Genesis 3:17-19. This is the curse that is declared to Adam. But, the "living bread" Jesus, brings us hope in the Scriptures. Jesus says, "…Truly, truly, I say to you, it is not Moses who has given you the bread out of heaven, but it is My Father who gives you the true bread out of heaven. For the bread of God is that which comes down out of heaven, and gives life to the world." (John 6:32-33) and "I am the living bread that came down out of heaven; if anyone eats of this bread, he will live forever; and the bread also which I will give for the life of the world is My flesh" (John 6:51). We can know eternal life through Jesus Christ alone. He is the true Bread; He is the One Who satisfies.

The manna that came from heaven, when Moses was leading the Israelites, only satisfied them temporarily, but Jesus satisfies forever. In the prayer that Jesus taught His disciples, He asks the Heavenly Father to "give us this day our daily bread" (see Matthew 6:11). When we do this we are asking for Him to meet all of our needs. It is interesting to notice that just prior to this we are told that the Father knows our needs before we ask (see Matthew 6: 8). All of our needs are met in Jesus, the Bread of life.

My comfort is found in knowing Him as my Satisfier, He meets my needs perfectly. He is the Bread of my life filling every emptiness and need, especially my biggest need of salvation from my sinfulness.

- *John 8:12 "I am the Light of the world . . . "*

Jesus declares, "I am the Light of the World." Doesn't it seem that fear increases in darkness? So many little children are fearful of the dark, but a small nightlight can dispel those fears. Light also helps us to find our way. Psalms 119:105 says, "Your Word is a lamp to my feet And a light to my path" (Psalm 119:105). Luke 2:32 tells us that Jesus was the Light from the beginning. Jesus manifests who God is, and 1 John 1:5 tells us that "God is Light". We are called to walk as children of light (see Ephesians 5:8).

The Light of the World brings me comfort, because He and His Word lead me; He shows me the way. The dark is not dark to me because He is my guide. Even through the valleys and the shadows He brings light to my path, so that I might know my way.

- *John 10:9 "I am the door, if anyone enters through Me, he will be saved and will go in and out and find pasture."*

In Chapter 1 of this book, the portion titled *Digging Deeper and Defining* The Sheep and His Shepherd we learned about how the shepherd laid his body across the opening of the cave or corral where he brought his flock at night. This is a picture of "the door" John refers to in this verse.

My comfort lies in knowing that Jesus is the door to heaven for me as I believe in Him. Hebrew 4:15-16 (AMP) helps us to better understand even more of what we have when we trust in Jesus:

> "For we do not have a High Priest Who is unable to understand *and* sympathize *and* have a shared feeling with our weaknesses and infirmities *and* liability to the assaults of temptation, but One Who has been tempted in every respect as we are, yet without sinning. Let us then fearlessly *and* confidently *and* boldly draw near to the throne of grace (the throne of God's unmerited favor to us sinners), that we may receive mercy [for our failures] and find grace to help in good time for every need [appropriate help and well-timed help, coming just when we need it.]"

I can depend on the grace I have through Jesus the Door to go to God the Father and then receive the help I need (appropriate help, well-timed help, coming just when I need it) for this life. What great comfort that brings to me.

- *John 10:11 "I am the good shepherd . . . "*

Here we return to David's view of the Lord in Psalm 23. We have previously discussed the role of the shepherd and the experience of the sheep. We learned that our Shepherd protects us, gives us rest, satisfies us, gives us eternal life, and teaches us to know His presence so we are not afraid, and He provides for us. I have comfort in the belonging I find in Him, in His care of me, and in His provision for me, and protection of me.

- *John 11:25 "I am the resurrection and the life . . . "*

Jesus has overcome the power of death and gives us life. The apostle Paul tells us:

> "But God, being rich in mercy, because of His great love with which He loved us, even when we were dead in our transgressions, made us alive together with Christ (by grace you have been saved), and raised us up with Him and seated us with Him in the heavenly *places* in Christ Jesus." (Ephesians 2:4-6)

Paul says, "For if we have become united with *Him* in the likeness of His death, certainly we shall be *in the likeness* of His resurrection" (Romans 6:5). We can find great comfort in knowing that as believers we receive eternal life and can look forward to our own resurrection when Jesus returns for us. David knew about this as well, in Psalm 17:15 he says, "As for me, I shall behold Your face in righteousness; I will be satisfied with Your likeness when I awake." We are promised that our bodies will be transformed to make us like His (see Philippians 3:21). Revelation 20:6 tells us that we who have "part in the first resurrection" will reign with Christ for a thousand years. The promises of future hope given, also gives much comfort as we struggle through this life. What joy we have to look forward to as we think about living eternally with our Lord and Savior.

- *John 14:6" I am the way, and the truth; and the life . . . "*

As we discussed in Chapter 3 of this book, God has direction for us, the paths of righteousness, He desires that we keep His commandments, live obediently, and walk in His ways (Deuteronomy 8:6). His way is "THE WAYS OF LIFE" (Acts 2:28) as well as "the way of salvation" (Acts 16:17). As we study the Word, we learn the truth, and should seek to obey it, as well as to speak it. Abundant and everlasting life is found in Christ alone. What great comfort we have in knowing that we can find all of this through our relationship with Christ Jesus.

- *John 15:1 "I am the true vine…"*

In chapter 15 of John we learn of the relationship between the vine—the Lord and the branches—us. There are two kinds of branches, those that are fruitful, and those that are not fruitful. We can only bear fruit as we remain attached to the vine. When the branch is no longer attached to the vine, it no longer has life and no longer can bear fruit. Our fruitfulness is evident in how we live our lives, by what our character is like, whether our lives demonstrate integrity and how we are maturing in our walk with the Lord, growing in the knowledge and wisdom of Him. All of these are ways that demonstrate that we are abiding, dwelling as attached branches. Great comfort is found in abiding, the Word promises us that as we abide we will receive answers to prayer. Jesus says, "You did not choose Me but I chose you, and appointed you that you would go and bear fruit, and *that* your fruit would remain, so that whatever you ask of the Father in My name He may give to you" (John 15:16).

It is in abiding in Him that His Word fills us, transforms our will and makes us more like Him. When we go to Him in prayer, we find our prayers answered because we have asked according to His will. I shared how I felt the Lord impress "But I am here" on my heart, I realize now the comfort the Lord had for me in Christ's "I am" statements and how they helped me to better understand the comfort of his presence. It is in personalizing the Word and taking it to heart that the Lord meets us in our neediness, whatever that might be. The presence of the Lord is my comfort in the painful, fearful, lonely, and hurtful times of life. The Psalmist says, "This is my comfort and consolation in my affliction; That Your word has revived me and given me life; Psalm 119:50 (AMP).Times of neediness come frequently to our lives, but I think all too often the noise of the day, the clutter of life blinds us to Him, and His presence. Our need for Him to revive us and to give us life is apparent. We have to learn to be intentional about planning to reach for Him because times for solitude do not occur without planning.

Reaching:
For Him in Solitude

Today our lives are often too frantic and frenzied to allow us quiet time alone to search our hearts in the presence of our Creator God— quiet time with the truthful beam of the Holy Spirit enlightening the darkness of our souls. Life is so stressful, our calendars so crammed, and our minds so racing. When do we find peace within? When do we get to know self in the light of the way God sees us? When do we find out what He wants for us? When do we seek His direction and guidance?

In 1 Kings 19:1-17 we read about Elijah in ministry at the mountain top and in the pit of depression. We see Elijah is at his wit's end, he is exhausted, full of fear, stressed and feeling used, maybe even abandoned and alone. We all get to this place at some time in our lives. He, too, was in need of comfort. Elijah decides he needs to get away from it all, for his personal protection and because he is just done. He decides his best choice is simply to die under a juniper tree and he tells God, this is it, I've had it. I can't do it anymore. He doesn't ask for energy, refreshment or help, he just asks to die and get it over. Some days are like that; we just want to crawl back in bed under the covers and die—or fly far, far away to a remote island to get away from the pressures of life. Sometimes we don't even remember that God is in this life with us. We forget that He is the God of all comfort. We just attempt to find our own form of relief from life.

The amazing thing is that God doesn't leave Elijah alone. How reassuring is that? When we get down and out, God doesn't walk out the door and say, "see you later, loser." Look at God. He sends an angel to minister to Elijah's most human needs. Then He lets Elijah have what he needs. The Lord brings him comfort in the form of food and drink and allows him to rest some more.

How have you felt the Lord minister to you when you are lying under your juniper tree? Once Elijah has rested and eaten, Elijah journeys to Mount Horeb and finds a cave in which to lodge. He gets there, and God asks him what he is doing there. Elijah is dead honest. Elijah tells God exactly where he is in life at that moment. I think this is an important lesson that we can learn from Elijah— we can lay it on the line with God. This is what's happening, this is how I feel. Where are you at in your life? How do you feel? What is going on? Is the juniper tree looking pretty good? Tell the Lord.

Elijah tells God what is going on in his life and God tells him to stand on the mount before the Lord. Do you think God noticed that Elijah hadn't asked Him for anything yet? Even so, God knew Elijah needed His presence. In His presence we find comfort, we find all that we need. God allows the chaos of the strong, damaging wind, earthquake, and a fire to occur. These are all fearful and powerful, as our God is. I can't help but think that God is saying to Elijah, have you forgotten who I am? I am the Almighty, all powerful, sovereign God Who can do anything.

How very human. How often do we forget who God is and what He can do in the midst of our lives? Anyone of these things could have killed Elijah in a moment. Elijah waits for God. Are you waiting for God in the storms of your life? What do you expect His presence to be like? When you wait for God, what do you look for?

God wasn't in the wind, the earthquake, or the fire. SILENCE! Then Elijah hears a still small voice and he knew it was God. He knew God's voice. Psalm 46:10 (KJV) says, "Be still, and know that I am God…"

Be still! It was in the stillness, in the silence and in his solitude, that Elijah heard God, and he knew God's voice. He wrapped his face and went out from the cave and God asked him again what he was doing there. And again, Elijah tells him. Nothing has changed. God prepared and nourished him, He allowed him to rest and to be ready for the journey, but, despite the comfort God has given, in Elijah's mind, nothing has changed. His circumstances remained the same. It must have seemed hopeless to Elijah.

Life gets that way sometimes. Hopeless. The circumstances of life can be so overwhelming and finally we collapse. We give up control and we plain give up. It is then God can work. It is then God shows us both who He is and what He can do. God listens to Elijah's desperation, and then God instructs him as to what he should do. Elijah goes in obedience and does what he is told. God listens. He hears our hearts, our need for comfort or whatever we need. In fact, He knows our needs before we ask. He knows the desperation of our human souls and He knows where we need to go and what we need to do. He is Wisdom and He grants wisdom to those who ask. James 1:5 says: "But if any of you lacks wisdom, let him ask of God, who gives to all generously and without reproach, and it will be given to him."

Elijah went away to die and God met him in his need. God knows exactly where we are at, emotionally, physically and spiritually. He is omniscient. It is easy to forget who He is, yet He tells us to know Him. He tells us what He offers to us in His Word.

In repentance and rest we find salvation, in quietness and trust we find strength (see Isaiah 30:15). God didn't come to Elijah in the wind, the earthquake, or the fire. He came in the still small voice.

The Lord strengthens and comforts us as he did Elijah when we are quiet before Him, willing to trust in Him, giving up our constant need to control. How do you seek to know Him? And if you don't seek Him, how can you expect peace of mind? We must come to Him. And then be silent and wait in His presence for Him to guide us, to direct us, to lead us or comfort us. He is faithful. He desires for us to look to Him, to look for Him. As we learn to know Him, we learn to trust Him and we choose to seek Him more and more, because we see Him working out all things for our good.

Whether you feel like lying down and dying under your juniper tree or just desire to walk more closely in His will, take time to be still and in your silence and solitude see Him, hear Him, and know Him.

Yes, *even though I walk through the valley of the shadow of death*, whatever that darkness is to me, *I will fear no evil* because the Lord is present with me. The great I AM never leaves me, He is present to protect (*rod*) and guide *(staff)*. *Your rod and your staff, they comfort me.* Knowing this guidance and protection of my Shepherd is with me day in and day out. I am comforted.

SOLITUDE

Sitting in His holy presence
Open to the Spirit's guide
Learning of His perfect will
Insight gained in my abide
Truths received in prayerful silence
Unending wisdom for His bride
Diligent to seek His leading
Enriched in Him and satisfied.

Questions:
For Life Application:

1. When in your life have you sensed a desperate need for comfort? By what methods have you tried to fill that need?

2. What are your deepest fears?

3. Which of the "I am" titles of Jesus bring you the most comfort at this point in your life? And why?

4. Do you take time for solitude?

5. How has the Lord ministered to you as you lay "under your juniper tree"?

6. Do you know God's voice? What has He been speaking to your heart?

7. How will you seek to find the comfort of solitude in the
    Lord's presence today?

Chapter 5

Anointed: Prepared for Service

Psalm 23:5 (ESV) "You prepare a table before me in the presence of my enemies; you anoint my head with oil; my cup overflows."

"You prepare a table before me in the presence of my enemies . . . "

Even in the midst of battle, even in the presence of enemies, the Lord sets out a feast before us. He calls us to know the safety and protection that is in Him and to partake from the fullness of His provision. The shepherd brings his sheep to a pasture for grazing. The Scriptures tell us "He causes the grass to grow for the cattle, And vegetation for the labor of man, So that he may bring forth food from the earth, And wine which makes man's heart glad, So that he may make *his* face glisten with oil, And food which sustains man's heart" (Psalm 104:14-15). Our Good Shepherd leads us, His sheep, to a great feast; He makes available all that we need. How beautiful the Lord's table, the place of fellowship, the place of communion, and the place where we are nourished.

There is rarely if ever a time or place in life, free of worries, free of struggles, free of stress, free of something warring against us. The Lord calls us to His banquet, to celebrate His goodness and be filled in whatever state we are in. He brings His sheep to *green pastures* and *still waters.*

The Lord knows our helplessness (Psalm 41:1-2) and He knows our needs. He is our shield and our strength (Psalm 18:1-3). Christ, our Savior reaches to us in love; He calls us and welcomes us. We are drawn to Him— drawn to the cross, drawn to the table. We are invited out of God's mercy, and welcomed in hospitality, the banquet is before us. *"You prepare a table before me, in the presence of my enemies."* The sheep ate in the pasture and drank of the quiet water provided by the shepherd in the presence of their enemies. The shepherd was their protector as they ate and drank. The Lord our Shepherd also prepares a table filled with His goodness throughout our lives where we are invited, and it too is in the presence of our enemies. He is our protector at the banquet.

Digging Deeper and Defining:
The Saint's Anointing

"...You anoint my head with oil . . . "

The shepherd of the flock found pasture for the flock and made sure for the safety of the animals. One precaution the shepherd took is anointing the sheep with oil. This was done for the sheep's protection from insects and the healing of any wounds to guard them from becoming infected. Anointing was a common custom in David's culture, especially during festival times.[15]

The following clearly explains the idea behind anointing as well as its practical importance:

> The Hebrew word for the verb to anoint is *mashach* and is the root of messiah, which means "anointed one." The basic idea of anointing in the Old Testament culture is a hygienic practice of applying oil or grease to soften and protect the skin in a dry climate (Amos 6:16; compare Ps. 23:5 which uses a different verb for the same idea). It can be used of pouring or smearing. This would be very soothing and refreshing. Oil and grease were also used to protect wounds and aid their healing. In one place the verb is used of oiling a leather shield to keep it from cracking (Isa. 21:5), and in another place it refers to painting a house (Jer. 22:14).

---

[15] Gary T. Panell, "Psalm 23 from the Sheep's Perspective Compiled by Gary T. Panell" Found at: http://bible-christian.org/lit/psalm23fromasheepsperspective.html.

The specific practice of anointing by pouring oil on the head was used as a symbolic act for officially, designating and setting apart a person for a certain, public, leadership function in the community. It was a one-time event much like an inauguration or ordination. Things could also be sanctified or dedicated to a special purpose for God by anointing (Exodus. 29:36). The three kinds of leaders anointed for their ministries in the Old Testament were: priests, Exodus. 28:41; kings, 1 Sam. 10:1; and prophets, 1 Ki. 19:16. A major difference between Israel and the other nations was that when God had someone anointed or authorized for leadership He also provided the empowering of the Holy Spirit to do the job (1 Sam. 16:13; Isa. 61:1).

...All Christians are anointed, according to 2 Cor. 1:21; and 1 John 2:20, 27, and thus are authorized and empowered agents of God . . . the biblical concept of anointing is that all Christians are anointed, meaning they are all authorized and empowered agents of God. All have the Spirit within and thus the power of God can be released through them at any time that He wants to and the person is yielding. [16]

Scripture explains, "...He who establishes us with you in Christ and anointed us is God, who also sealed us and gave *us* the Spirit in our hearts as a pledge" (2 Corinthians 1:21). All who are in Christ are anointed together—all of us were given the same Holy Spirit, as a down payment of the resurrection. The Spirit will work through us, using His gifts in us to fulfill God's calling in each of our lives. Our calling from God leads us to walk in service

---

[16] Dr. Roger Cotton. "ANOINTING IN THE OLD TESTAMENT". Found at: http://www.agts.edu/faculty/faculty_publication/articles/cotton_anointing.pdf Used by permission.

to Him as His servants. Jesus is our perfect example when it comes to servanthood.

The Lord's Word/The Lord's Work: Jesus the Servant, Our Perfect Example

Paul explains the purpose of Jesus' servanthood: "For I say that Christ has become a servant to the circumcision on behalf of the truth of God to confirm the promises *given* to the fathers" (Romans 15:8). Jesus' life as a servant was to manifest to us, in flesh and blood, the faithfulness of God to His promises, to give us the hope of salvation.

Jesus gave up equality with God even though He was one with God and was in the form of God (see Philippians 2:6-7). He humbled Himself to take on human flesh. He chose to become a servant.

Jesus demonstrated the qualities of a perfect servant. As we grow in Christ-likeness our lives reflect them as well. Let's look at the servant qualities that Christ demonstrated.

A Christ-like servant demonstrates humility.

Humility means to be humble, which is defined as being modest, lowly, or unpretentious. One example of Jesus walking in *humility* is when He washed the disciple's feet in the Upper Room prior to His crucifixion (see John 13:1-20). Washing the feet of others was the job of the lowliest slave in those days.

John 13: 5 begins by saying, *"Then He poured water into the basin."* Jesus began the act of washing the feet of the disciples by *pouring* the water to get ready to cleanse them. Jesus *poured* out His lifeblood for us, to cleanse us from our sins. Isaiah tells us about the Suffering Servant as follows:

> "Therefore, I will allot Him a portion with the great, And He will divide the booty with the strong; Because He *poured out* Himself to death, And was numbered with the transgressors; Yet He Himself bore the sin of many, And interceded for the transgressors" (Isaiah 53:12; emphasis mine)

Jesus *poured* the water; Jesus *poured* Himself, the ultimate sacrifice. He humbled Himself to wash the feet of the disciples. He humbled Himself to die on the cross. Being a Christ-like servant requires us to demonstrate humility in our lives as we interact and respond to those in our lives.

A Christ-like servant lives a life demonstrating selfless sacrifice.

In humility Christ died on the cross, *sacrificing* His life for us. It is at the cross that we come to see and know the fullness of God's grace. His grace is the basis for our service. It is out of His grace that we have our abilities, gifts, wealth, and talents. All of these are available for us to use in service to others as we live out our lives following the example of Christ.

We can emulate Christ's *selflessness*, the *sacrificial offering* of His life, by willingly sacrificing time, money, or whatever is required in order to serve another. The apostle Paul tells us, "Therefore I urge you, brethren, by the mercies of God, to present your bodies a living and holy sacrifice, acceptable to God, *which* is your spiritual service of worship" (Romans 12:1). When we pour out our lives in serving others in *selfless sacrifice* it requires willingness to surrender self as well as whatever we have to meet these needs.

Living sacrificially is an area that is difficult for me, especially when I am asked to give up "my time." I came to realize this as I was reading the book *A Journey to Victorious Prayer* by Bill Thrasher. In one of the chapters, the reader is asked to consider who their Isaac is. I reread the story of Abraham (see Genesis 22) and his willingness to sacrifice his only son Isaac. I began to contemplate what or whom it was that I was holding onto so tightly. What was I choosing not to lay on the altar before God? I came up with nothing. The next day as I felt led to call someone to meet them for lunch; I selfishly thought how I would rather hoard the time for myself. In fact, it became clear to me, how I always guarded my time. And I saw plainly then that "my time" was my Isaac. It seems like there is never enough time to do the things that I want to do. I constantly think of how I can save time to rest, read, or write. The Lord was showing me, how time, for me, was too often more important to me than serving Him. As I went to the Lord with this, He made clear His promises. He knows my needs (Matthew 6:8), He offers me rest (Matthew 11:28-30), He promises to give me the desires of my heart as I delight in Him (Psalm 37:4), and He hears my prayers (1 John 5:14-15). One by one, all of my reasons for hoarding time were wiped out. I told Him that I needed to give Him my time and asked Him to help me use each moment according to His will and purpose. I continue to struggle with this area and must continually bring it to the Lord in prayer. Abraham was willing to sacrifice Isaac, his long promised son. I want to be willing to sacrifice my time and be available to do what the Lord asks of me. Who or what is your Isaac? What do you need to willingly sacrifice to be a Christ-like servant?

A Christ-like servant touches others with His love.

John 13:5 goes on: H*e washed the disciple's feet.* In washing their feet, Jesus *touched* His disciples with that incredible servant love enriching their lives forever. 1 Corinthians 13:4-7 describes fully what the *love* of God is like, true *agape love*:

> "Love is patient, love is kind *and* is not jealous; love does not brag *and* is not arrogant, does not act unbecomingly; it does not seek its own, is not provoked, does not take into account a wrong *suffered,* does not rejoice in unrighteousness, but rejoices with the truth; bears all things, believes all things, hopes all things, endures all things."

We often hear these verses shared at weddings. I think of a wedding as an occasion for a man and a woman to commit their love and their lives to each other. Being a Christ-like servant is similar because as a servant we are to be committed to live life out in loving others in the same way that Jesus did. This kind of serving is acting with a willingness to touch another life deeply, even to the point of tenderly caressing smelly, dirty feet. This is the kind of service for which we have been anointed. Christ's humility, selflessness, and love led Him to obedience, which made Him willing to die on the cross (Philippians 2:8).

A Christ-like servant walks in obedience to God's will.

Jesus came into the world to carry out God's will. He was willing to go to all lengths to deny His own will, in order to do the Father's will. He tells His disciples, "For I have come down from heaven not to do My own will *and* purpose but to do the will *and* purpose of Him Who sent me" John 6:38 (AMP). *Obedience* is rarely an easy choice. It is typically difficult and, we often want to take a different path. *Obedience* does not always seem like the best idea to us nor is it usually what is popular according to the world's standards. *Obedience* is the way of righteousness that our Shepherd leads us. *Obedience*, for Christ, meant walking in servant sandals to the cross to suffer.

A Christ-like servant is willing to suffer.

Isaiah 53:3-5 tells us some of what our Suffering Servant experienced in our place:

> "He was despised and forsaken of men, A man of sorrows and acquainted with grief; And like one from whom men hide their face He was despised, and we did not esteem Him. Surely our griefs He Himself bore. And our sorrows He carried; Yet we ourselves esteemed Him stricken, Smitten of God, and afflicted. But He was pierced through for our transgressions, He was crushed for our iniquities; The chastening for our well-being fell upon Him, And by His scourging we are healed."

106

Yet in the midst of this suffering even then He "did not open His mouth" (Isaiah 53:7). He didn't retaliate, or argue or seek revenge. Peter tells us:

> "… to the degree that you share the sufferings of Christ, keep on rejoicing, so that also at the revelation of His glory you may rejoice with exultation. If you are reviled for the name of Christ, you are blessed, because the Spirit of glory and of God rests on you… Therefore, those also who suffer according to the will of God shall entrust their souls to a faithful Creator in doing what is right" (1 Peter 4:13-14, 19).

Sharing in the *sufferings* of Christ is a part of life as a Christ-follower. Suffering is to be expected. Peter was talking about the persecution that touches the lives of Christians because of their beliefs. What might this mean for us? It may mean people putting us down, or abusing us verbally. It may mean being mocked for our faith or slandered. And, although we are not very familiar with this happening in our country, it may even mean being tortured physically or dying for one's faith. We are to look to God in His faithfulness during times of suffering and find joy in doing His will no matter the outcome. The apostle Paul tells us, "For to you it has been granted on behalf of Christ, not only to believe in Him, but also to suffer for His sake" (Philippians 1:29).

It seems as though any *suffering* that touches our lives always brings us to respond with "why" or "why me"? We don't understand. It doesn't seem fair. We don't want to have to go through the pain or difficulty, yet God uses suffering to fulfill His purposes. Through *suffering* the Lord strengthens our faith; He makes us more like Jesus, as well as making us more committed to Him.

So far, being a Christ-like servant sounds difficult and painful, but it doesn't end here, our faith is worth it all because of the hope we have in Christ. What joy fills our hearts.

A Christ-like servant finishes with joy because of the hope within.

John 13:5 ends by telling us how *Jesus wipes the disciples' feet with a towel.* He finished His work by wiping His disciple's feet. He finished the work on the cross in order that He can wipe away our tears when we join Him in heaven. Revelation 7:17 says "…and God will wipe every tear from their eyes." As Christians, we have this hope to look forward to; it is a promise that fills our hearts with *joy.* Our lives on this earth can be lived out with an eternal perspective that nothing can destroy. We can serve with *joy* because our hope is eternal.

> *Jesus has given us a beautiful example of how to live as a servant. We have learned from Him that a servant demonstrates humility, lives a life of selfless sacrifice, touches others with love, walks in obedience to God's will, is willing to suffer and finishes with joy because of the Hope that is within.*

As Christians we know that Christ chose servanthood in order to bring glory to the Father and we as His children also should purpose to do the same. How will you begin to follow His example today? He has anointed our heads with oil that we might serve Him. We have seen how Christ fulfilled His Father's will for His life as a servant, as His servant we should follow Christ's example. We also need to find out His will and purpose for our lives.

Reaching:
To Find His Purpose

"…My cup overflows…"

As a Christian, I think one of the most important questions to ask ourselves is, "What is the Lord's purpose for my life here on earth?" We are each called to the Great Commission (see Matthew 28:19-20). Yet I am speaking of a purpose that is still the Great Commission, but is unique for each individual. As I look back at how the Lord led me to know His purpose for my life, I see how the Lord took my depression to bring me to a place in my life where I was fervent in my desire to really know Him, to know what His Word had to say to me, and to want to know how He wanted me to live for Him— to really seek His will. He led me to desire to find satisfaction in Him. It is amazing to me that the reality of His purpose for me became real to me in the pain and grief of my depression, and the neediness that filled me. I only learned God's purpose for myself as I sought to grow in knowing Him more and began to desire to walk in holiness. And then, as my heart was turned to Him, I reached hungrily for Him to feed me. As I grew in a more intimate relationship with my Lord, I learned to hear the wind-words of His Spirit whispering to my spirit. He led me with His instructions through His Word, through the sermons of others, through my prayer-life communicating with Him, and in fellowship with other Christians to walk in rhythm with His Spirit. The Holy Spirit used His power to transform me, and my desires. He led me to learn of the spiritual gifts He had given to me.

In God's Word, Jesus often demonstrates, by example, what He desires for us to take to heart and to live out in our lives. In the example of feet washing, He demonstrates His humility, His love, and His desire to touch others in service. As we seek to emulate Jesus in our lives, we are led to live a life of selflessness. And in learning to walk in Christ-likeness we ultimately find joy and satisfaction. Part of our personal joy and satisfaction comes from the fact that we can truly know that we are bringing glory to God. When you love someone, you desire to please him or her, and bring honor to his or her name. In our love for the Lord, our goal should be to glorify His name in all that we do (see 1 Corinthians 10:31).

In time, I found that some of my pain actually led me to areas]of passion. As we consider our lives, we all have certain desires and passions that fill us. Our passions reflect our deepest yearnings. When we are living out our passions, we are somehow energized. We do that passionate thing because we love to do it. I found that my pain, mostly the loneliness within, led me first to deep intimacy with the Lord, and then to acknowledge my personal need for depth in my relationships with others. I was brought beyond the place of living in independence out of fear. The grief of my depression and the resulting joy of my intimate with the Lord led me to a deeper love for others who were in pain and in need of comfort. Isaiah foretells of Jesus' ministry in the verses that follow. This passage resonated with my heart for ministry also.

> "The Spirit of the Lord GOD is upon me, Because the LORD has anointed me, To bring good news to the afflicted; He has sent me to bind up the brokenhearted, To proclaim liberty to captives, And freedom to prisoners; To proclaim the favorable year of the LORD And the day of vengeance of our God; To comfort all who mourn, To grant those who mourn *in* Zion, Giving them a garland instead of ashes, The oil of gladness instead of mourning, The mantle of praise instead of a spirit of fainting So they will be called oaks of righteousness, The planting of the LORD, that He may be glorified." (Isaiah 61:1-3)

Out of my pain, the Lord led me to understand what my life mission was. I personalized these verses as what my purpose would be in fulfilling the mission I felt led to make real in my life. Jesus repeats some of these verses in Luke 4:18, words that were fulfilled in Him.

My mission statement and purpose statements follow:

My mission is to encourage and minister in grace to women (especially hurting women) and build them up in love by being a servant of the Lord.

My purpose in fulfilling my mission is to:

1. *To bring good news to the meek and poor in spirit by sharing the Gospel with the lost.*

2. *To bring comfort to the brokenhearted whose lives have been touched with abandonment, rejection, replacement, or loneliness by offering compassion, understanding, and connection.*

3. *To announce release for captives and freedom for prisoners; those who are imprisoned in unhealthy relationships, in bondage to unforgiving hearts, or oppressed with emotional woundedness by leading them to the liberty found in Christ Jesus.*

4. *To share the Lord's favor with those who are mourning (grieving deep losses of irreplaceable people that have left holes in their hearts), by touching their lives with His love acted out in the service of listening and meeting their needs as the Lord directs.*

5. *To bring promise of how, out of ashes, mourning and despair, the Lord can lead them to beauty, joy and praise, by way of sharing my testimony as I describe how feeding on His faithfulness has led me to abundant life in Him alone.*

Our purpose gives us a grid to sift through the stuff of life that comes at us from all angles, seeking us to be involved, to do and to respond to. As we learn our personal God-given purpose(s) we find a way to better know what our goals should be, and what we should choose to do. It is amazing to me that our loving Lord can take all of our passions, our pain, and our successes and mold them together in us to be used for His purpose. The grief of depression that has touched me deeply, led me to compassion, and to comfort others in similar pain. He leads us to live a life with a mission to bring glory to Him. The Lord filled *my cup to overflowing* as His purpose for me leads to so many amazing blessings.

As you read My Life Experience you will see more clearly how this was made real in my life.

My Life Experience:
Growing through the Pain

My deep depression was a very difficult time for me. It was a time of many tears, much pain, agony, and anguish. To give you a brief look into my heart at that time I want to share a few of the poems I wrote during the time of my depression.

Abandoned to Anguish

She felt dead inside,
as if her blood had been sucked out,
and her veins filled with water,
then froze within her,
leaving her cold and lifeless.
She was so alone,
no warmth touched her,
neediness for love overwhelmed her.
Her despair spilled out in tears.
Pain filled her life.
She had no desire to go on.
She felt so empty.
She saw only blackness,
Her breath was shallow.
Life felt like a burden,
weighing heavy on her heart.

Her agony went unnoticed,
abandoned to anguish,
all hope was lost,
like the blood from her veins.
The hours seemed endless.
she only wanted to die,
to feel no more.
She could find no reason to live.
Death alone would numb her.
Death alone would bring her peace,
and end her desperation.

Suffocating

There's nothing left inside,
only stark emptiness remains.
Pain pierces through my heart,
as a continual reminder of,
the desperation I'm left with.
The wound is ripped open raw,
by the abandonment of love,
the agony of loss tortures me.
I am suffocating in this tomb.
Lying here so lost and lifeless,
no air to sustain my existence.
There's just no life within,
only unending neediness,
neediness for healing in my soul,
neediness for life to be breathed into,
the depths of my innermost being.
There's nothing left inside,
only stark emptiness remains.
Left to die, buried and forgotten.
My pain overwhelms me,
and I am so very much alone.
Abandoned and suffocating in this tomb.

Beyond Help

You can't hear me breathe.
I have been beaten by deep pain,
in too much agony to gasp for air,
only tears fall without effort.
Hopelessness is all that remains.
I am empty and too far beyond help.
I am left alone in my sadness.
Life?
I no longer look for it,
I no longer want it.
My neediness will be buried with me.
No one can fill my heart,
it's too broken to even hold hope.
Earth, I feel you beneath me,
open up and swallow me in,
I lay waiting only for death.

I spent many hours journaling, pouring out the hurt in my heart. I spent time reading the Psalmist's laments. I cried and cried. I could only see the dark side of things. I couldn't understand how anyone could laugh. It seemed like the intensity of the pain within my heart should have stopped the world from turning or at least have kept the sun from shining. And in the midst of the months of my depression I wanted nothing more than to be rid of the inner pain. I had no idea what the Lord was doing within me.

The Lord drew me to deep intimacy with Him and in doing so, He changed the insides of me. He changed me from running, from always seeking to be busy to wanting solitude and silence. I had made sure that I was busy so I didn't have to feel and think because that often made me aware of the pain within. However, as intimacy with the Lord grew and healing took place I desired to go to that quiet place; it was okay to be alone because I finally realized I wasn't really alone anymore. He (the Lord) met me in His Word. He changed me, from only wanting to escape my own thoughts and feelings to wanting to understand my feelings and thoughts as they relate to His Word. He changed me from wanting to run away from the neediness within to a willingness to acknowledge my neediness and take it to Him, and expect Him to meet me in that place of neediness. I learned to desire connection and relationship. Rather than being content with superficial relationships I found satisfaction in sharing deeply, in connecting my fear of sharing who I was and what I felt, lessened. My trust in the Lord helped

me to be more secure in opening up with others. I grew to a
deeper level of trust in the Lord and the knowledge of His love for
me. Intimately the Lord drew me to fill my heart, giving me the
desire to want to share the healing and joy that He brought to me.
Along with those changes and new desires within me, He opened
up doors of opportunity for me to share. He led me to other
women who needed to hear portions of my life story as
encouragement or needed to be mentored as they themselves were
struggling in their walks with the Lord, in finding intimacy with
Him. He also led me to do retreats. In the retreats He allowed me
to enjoy deep connection, He revealed the wisdom of His Word to
me and helped me to share it in ways relevant to the needs and
hurts in women's lives. He allowed me to serve Him and He
blessed me in my obedience. Years later, He led me to
understanding what this book was to be and pulled it together, as
He has pulled my life together. He took me through a time of
suffering to learn how I am to live in service to Him. He showed
me truths throughout this time and He taught me of the
magnitude of His love and compassion—*my cup overflows*. What an
awesome God we have, who sees me (see Genesis 16:13-14) and
thinks on me (see Psalm 40:17) and cares for me (see 1Peter 5:7).
He led me to delight in Him and showed me desires of my heart
that I never knew I had (see Psalm 37:4). Then He brought me
great joy as He made those desires a reality and He continues to
fulfill my desires in new and unbelievable ways. The following is a

poem that I wrote in response to what I realized came out of my pain and the awareness of how incredibly beautiful and amazing the Lord's work in my life had been. To Him be the glory, great things He has done!

Pain's Preciousness…God's Pearl

Pain embedded in my heart
Initially an irritant
I want to rid it from within
Soon a tender part of me
Needing protection
Losing it means greater emptiness
Pain wrapped in a shield
Becoming a comfort
Something to cling tightly to
So precious to my soul
At last revealed
Pain glistens in beauty
God's purpose demonstrated
Others lives touched
With the glory of His love
Pain never wasted
My hearts passion fulfilled
My hearts longings satisfied
These realized and defined
In Him and by Him
From pain's preciousness
God creates a pearl

Questions:
For Life Application:

1. How are you living your life as a servant?

2. Do you see the Lord developing His Christ-like servant qualities in you?

3. Do you see evidence of how the difficult times draw you into deeper relationship with the Lord?

4. What are your passions? Do you see the Lord leading you via your pain and your passions to His purpose for your life?

Chapter 6
The Full Satisfaction of His Presence

Psalm 23:6 (ESV) "Surely goodness and mercy shall follow me all the days of my life, and I shall dwell in the house of the LORD forever."

Great is Thy Faithfulness

Life is filled with both seasons of pain and those of joy; the Lord doesn't waste either. As David completes this psalm, we find him encouraged by the Lord's work in his life. David feeds on the Lord's faithfulness (see Psalm 37:3). He realizes that God's lovingkindness is a mercy that never fails (Psalm 106:1). The Lord has made this real in David's life.

Do you know the work of the Lord's mercy in your life?

His mercy is always ready and as never-ending as His love. It is a mercy that we can depend upon:

> God is an inexhaustible *fountain of mercy, the Father of mercies.*
> Note, We all owe it to the sparing mercy of *God that we are not*
> consumed. ...These rivers of mercy run fully and constantly, but
> never run dry...*his tender mercies are over all his works*; all his
> creatures taste of his goodness. But he is in a particular manner
> good *to those that wait for him, to the soul that seeks him.* Note. While
> trouble is prolonged and deliverance is deferred, we must
> patiently wait for God and his gracious returns to us. While we
> *wait for him* by faith, we must *seek him* by prayer: our *souls* must
> *seek him*, else we do not seek so as to find. Our seeking will help
> to keep up our waiting. And to those who thus wait and seek
> God will be gracious; he will show them his *marvelous*
> *lovingkindness*.[17]

Our Lord does not disappoint. As we recognize the Lord's
faithfulness we come to realize more about the assuredness of His
plans for goodness and mercy to us. It is David, himself, who says
of the Lord, "Yet you are enthroned as the Holy One; you are the
praise of Israel. In you our fathers put their trust; they trusted and
you delivered them. They cried to you and were saved; in you they
trusted and were not disappointed" Psalm 22:3-5 (NIV). The Lord
desires that we are satisfied in Him; He pursues us for this reason.
Surely goodness and mercy will follow me all the days of my life. The verb

---

[17] These files are public domain and are a derivative of an electronic edition that is
available on the Christian Classics Ethereal Library website.
  Henry, Matthew. "Complete Commentary on Lamentations 3". "Matthew Henry Complete
Commentary on the Whole Bible".
http://www.studylight.org/com/mhccom/view.cgi?book=la&chapter=003 1706.

"radaf" (translated as "follows") means to pursue. He pursues us with His goodness and mercy:

> The use of רָדַף (radaf, "pursue, chase") with וְחֶסֶד טוֹב (tov vakhesed, "goodness and faithfulness") as subject is ironic. This is the only place in the entire OT where either of these nouns appears as the subject of this verb רָדַף (radaf, "pursue"). This verb is often used to describe the hostile actions of enemies. One might expect the psalmist's enemies (see v. 5) to chase him, but ironically God's "goodness and faithfulness" (which are personified and stand by metonymy for God himself) pursue him instead. The word "pursue" is used outside of its normal context in an ironic manner and creates a unique, but pleasant word picture of God's favor (or a kind God) "chasing down" the one whom he loves. [18]

David learns repeatedly throughout his life of the many benefits of the Lord (see Psalm 103). The Lord satisfies David's desires with good things. The Lord works His righteousness and justice in times of oppression. Here, in Psalm 23, David also recognizes how the Lord has been gracious to him; the Lord has fed him, led him, restored him, strengthened him, preserved him, and blessed him with much. He knows and trusts that because the realities of God's faithfulness throughout his life illustrate that His favor will continue. The Word tells us that the Lord does not change (Malachi 3:6).

---

[18]Scripture and/or notes quoted by permission. Quotations designated (NET) are from the NET Bible® copyright ©1996-2006 by Biblical Studies Press, L.L.C. http://bible.org All rights reserved.

As we travel this journey of life, we too can be assured that His goodness and mercy will pursue us forever. The Lord wants so much for us to delight in knowing His faithfulness. He pursues us with His mercy and His love desiring to lead us to have a heart of worship, leading us *from wilderness to worship*. What is it that leads you to respond with worship before God? Do you know the Father's loving-kindness and mercy in your life?

> The mercies of God are new every morning, they continue all the day long; temporal goodness abides as long as life lasts, and ends with it; and spiritual blessings are for ever, they are the gifts of God which are without repentance.[19]

Digging Deeper and Defining:
Spiritual Blessings all the Days of My Life

In Ephesians 1:4-14 Paul spells out for us an array of spiritual blessings that we can count on:

> "just as *He chose us* in Him before the foundation of the world, that we would be holy and blameless before Him. In love *He predestined us* to adoption as sons through Jesus Christ to Himself, according to the kind intention of His will, to the praise

---

[19] John Gill's Exposition of the Bible is in the public domain and may be freely used and distributed. Found at http://www.biblestudytools.com/commentaries/gills-exposition-of -the-bible/psalms-23/

of the glory of His grace, which He freely bestowed on us in the Beloved.

In Him we have redemption through His blood, the forgiveness of our trespasses, according to the riches of His grace which He lavished on us.

In all wisdom and insight ***He made known to us the mystery of His will,*** according to His kind intention which He purposed in Him with a view to an administration suitable to the fullness of the times, *that is*, the summing up of all things in Christ, things in the heavens and things on the earth.

In Him also we have obtained an inheritance, having been predestined according to His purpose who works all things after the counsel of His will, to the end that ***we who were the first to hope in Christ would be to the praise of His glory***.

In Him, you also, after listening to the message of truth, the gospel of your salvation—having also believed, ***you were sealed in Him with the Holy Spirit of promise***, who is given as a pledge of our inheritance, with a view to the redemption of *God's own* possession, to the praise of His glory." (emphasis mine)

These spiritual blessings belong to us because of our identification with and position in Christ.

Let's look more closely at the blessings we have in Him.

• We were chosen "…in Him before the foundation of the world" (vs. 4).

We were chosen by the Lord to be holy and without blame. He

chose us through the gospel, that we might gain the glory of Christ (2 Thessalonians 2:13b-14).

- We have been "predestined…to adoption" (vs. 5).

God foreordained that we be adopted. We are adopted as members of the family of God.

- We have "redemption through His blood" and "forgiveness of our trespasses" (vs. 6).

The guilt of our sinfulness has been removed. We have been freed from the slavery of sin. We have the acceptance of our Heavenly Father because of what Jesus did on the cross for us. The apostle Paul tells us that "[All] are justified and made upright *and* in right standing with God, free *and* gratuitously by His grace (His unmerited favor and mercy), through the redemption which is [provided] in Christ Jesus" Romans 3:24 (AMP).

- We have been given the knowledge of the "mystery of His will" (vs. 9).

Paul shares our Heavenly Father's secret plan with us, to let us know what our future is:

"[This mystery] was never disclosed to human beings in past generations as it has now been revealed to His holy apostles (consecrated messengers) and prophets by the [Holy] Spirit. [It is this;] that the Gentiles are now to be fellow heirs [with the Jews], members of the same body and joint partakers [sharing]in the same divine promise in Christ Jesus through [their acceptance of] the glad tidings of (the Gospel)" Ephesians 3:5-6 (AMP).

- We have "obtained an inheritance" (vs. 11).

Peter gives explanation of our inheritance in these verses:

"Praise (honored, blessed) be the God and Father of our Lord Jesus Christ (the Messiah)! By His boundless mercy we have been born again to an ever-living hope through the resurrection of Jesus Christ from the dead. [Born anew] into an inheritance which is beyond the reach of change and decay [imperishable], unsullied and unfading, reserved in heaven for you, Who are being guarded (garrisoned) by God's power through [your] faith [till you fully inherit that final] salvation that is ready to be revealed [for you] in the last time." 1 Peter 1:3-5 (AMP)

- We have been "sealed with the Holy Spirit of promise" (vs. 13).

Our inheritance is kept for us by the Holy Spirit until we take possession of it. And all of this is for the purpose of bringing glory to God. He blesses us that we might glorify Him.

131

> Goodness and mercy follow [the believer] always—all the
> days of his life- the black days as well as the bright days, the days
> of fasting as well as the days of feasting, the dreary days of
> winter as well as the bright days of summer. Goodness supplies
> our needs and mercy blots out our sins. [20]

When this life on earth ends, we, as children of God, look
forward to eternal life with our Heavenly Father who gave Jesus to
die for us. What incredible joy and peace this brings to the heart of
the believer! No wonder David was so convinced of the Lord as
his deliverer and held such great hope for *dwelling in the presence of
God* in the future and *forever*. No wonder David desired to worship
the Lord forever!

The Lord's Word/The Lord's Work: Forever in Him

David completes verse six with knowing that he *will* "dwell in
the house of the Lord forever." Home. What a comfort that word
brings. Yet, this *home* means so much more, it means dwelling in
the presence of the Lord, being fully satisfied by His presence, not

---

[20] Charles Spurgeon. "Treasury of David." These files are public domain and are a
derivative of an electronic edition that is available on the Christian Classics Ethereal Library
website.
    Spurgeon, Charles H. "Commentary on Psalms 23:6". "C. H. Spurgeon's The Treasury of
David". http://www.studylight.org/com/tod/view.cgi?book=ps&chapter=023&verse=006 1865-
1885

just for a moment here or there as in this life but forever, constantly, without end.

David tells us that, "The Lord knows the days of the upright *and* blameless and their heritage will abide forever in Christ" Psalm 37:18 (AMP). Forever in Him, that is what David wanted and desired above all. Even those many years before our Savior's birth, death and resurrection David knows that only in God's presence could there be full satisfaction. David came to know the Lord's presence as he sat out in the fields guarding the sheep, as he led them besides the still waters and as he made them to lie down in the green pastures. He learned how to be in the secret places of the Lord's presence as he meditated on the Word of God that he had hid in his heart. There under the stars he came to really know the Lord and to know the satisfaction that His presence brings. And now he writes of dwelling there forever in his life, in his heart and finally in eternal life. David learned to know God's love and this makes him want to live in the Lord's presence continually.

The goodness of God is something to be enjoyed. David tells us of the greatness of God's love as he praised Him with these words:

> "How precious is Your steadfast love, O God! The children of men take refuge *and* put their trust under the shadow of your wings. They relish *and* feast on the abundance of Your house; and You cause them to drink of the stream of Your pleasures. For with You is the fountain of life, in Your light do we see

light. O continue Your loving-kindness to those who know You, Your righteousness (salvation) to the upright in heart." Psalm 36:7-10 (AMP)

Jesus the Light of the world gave His life for us and gave life to us because of the goodness and love of God. God has called us into union with Christ and into communion with Him. Our union and communion are eternal, forever. Once we have received Him into our hearts accepting His death and resurrection as payment for our sins we can be sure of all that we have in Him.

We seek to find satisfaction on the earth in various ways, with varied things and people, but when we clearly know His presence we see how all else lacks in satisfying. It is when we realize this, that we too look forward to dwelling forever in His presence and knowing the full satisfaction that this brings. We are told in John 14 of the Father's house and the many rooms there. Jesus tells us that He goes away to prepare a place for us and promises His return. It is in heaven that we will know truly, what it means to be satisfied in Him as we will truly rest in His presence and fully know His love:

> "For the Lord Himself will descend from heaven with a loud cry of summons, with the shout of an archangel, and with the blast of the trumpet of God. And those who have departed this life in Christ will rise first. Then we the living ones who remain [on the earth], shall simultaneously be caught up along with [the resurrected dead] in the clouds to meet the Lord in the air; and

so always (through the eternity of the eternities) we shall be with the Lord." 1 Thessalonians 4:16-17 (AMP)

There is that foreverness in the "always" in the description of that word as the "eternity of the eternities." Can you say with David that you too will dwell in the house of the Lord forever? This future hope helps me make it through the rough times. But every day I need to know more of His presence in my life.

My Life Experience:
Knowing More of His Presence in My Day

We as humans need to hold tight to the love we have found in life, those who have loved us are precious treasures to us and we hold them close in our hearts. We want them always in our lives. I have a sedum planted in my garden that was from my grandfather's (Opah's) garden. It is precious to me and next to it I have placed a small rock imprinted with the word "forever". Whenever I go out to my front border garden, I see that rock next to the plant and remember. I remember my Opah— our times together and especially his love for me. Sometimes I smile and at other times, tears fill my eyes, but always I somehow feel his presence because of the memories. Memories that may otherwise have not come to mind without that "stone" in my garden – it is a stone of remembrance. I have it there to remember my Opah and to remind myself that he lives on in my heart forever, because his love has grown to be a part of me.

We frequently set up memorials to those we love, or have lost, such as a picture, a special ornament on the Christmas tree, a piece of jewelry that we treasure—all to help us "remember" what we shared with that person and to feel their love in our lives. How much more important is it to know the Father's love and His presence throughout the course of our days? It is as we grow in knowing Him that we learn more and more of how we truly can be at "rest" in Him. The eyes of our hearts help us to constantly see Him as we go through our days, and remember who He is to us in this present life. What a difference that makes in our lives. There is a direct correlation between truly knowing His love, His faithfulness, the truth of His wisdom and our ability to cease from striving to rest in Him in the here and now.

Thinking about this has made me realize my need for some types of memorials in my daily life to help me be reminded of His presence. Somehow, the moments and hours of life get so busy it is too easy to be so preoccupied with the temporal that I forget the Eternal One. I need to be reminded to think on His faithfulness, to meditate on His goodness, to sing of His loving-kindness, and to be encouraged to seek the knowledge of His wisdom. Some memorials for me may be the practice of a little prayer in the middle of my day, or repeating a verse of a song as I do some mundane task. At other times, it is a small object that I keep in my pocket so I can touch it to be reminded to think of how He has shown me His love. For a while, I carried a small rock in my pocket and when I touched it I considered the strength I found in the Rock of my salvation. Being reminded of His presence and His promises help me to rest in Him throughout the stresses of my day. It is too easy to feel overwhelmed in this life. I know I need a little taste of heaven in each day just to help keep me going.

Reaching:
For Sabbath Rest:
A Little Taste of Heaven

Heaven is the Christian's place of eternal rest. It seems like my heart constantly cries out for something better in this life here on earth; I desire and need true rest. Life in this world is exhausting. Jesus calls to us and tells us to come and find rest in Him (Matthew 11:28-30). Do you need a little more heaven in your life today? I think that it is as we learn of Sabbath rest and live that out we can know a little taste of heaven in our lives.

I have found three principles that lead us to grow a heart of Sabbath rest.

1. Growing a heart for Sabbath rest requires knowing God's unlimited resources to give us inner strength for every area of our life.

In Ephesians chapter 3 Paul gives us a prayer, and it is in this prayer, we find a beginning place for growing a heart of Sabbath rest. Paul begins his prayer:

> "May He grant you out of the rich treasury of His glory to be strengthened *and* reinforced with mighty power in the inner man by the [Holy] Spirit [Himself indwelling your innermost being and personality]." Ephesians 3:16 (AMP)

Here we are told that the inherent power of God is available to us for our lives:

> …Believers in Christ need fresh supplies of strength to enable them to exercise grace, to perform duties, to resist Satan and his temptations, to oppose their corruptions, and to bear the cross, and undergo afflictions cheerfully, and to hold on and out the end; this is a blessing that comes from God, and is a gift of his free grace; a "grant" from him who is the strength of the lives of his people, of their salvation, of their hearts, and of the work of grace in their hearts: the means whereby the saints are strengthened by God, is "his Spirit", who strengthens them by

leading them to the fullness of grace and strength in Christ…[21]

I was helped to better understand what this mighty power is by this explanation:

> That He (God the Father) would grant (give) you according (agreeing with, in harmony with) to the riches (abundance) of His glory (power and majesty). We see that God the Father wants to give us something according to the abundance of His glory. What is it that He wants to give to us? His gift is for us to be strengthened with might through His Spirit in our inner man. …The word strengthened is the Greek word "krataioo". It literally means to add strength to, and make it stronger. For example, iron is strengthened by adding carbon to it while the iron is molten hot. The result is steel. God wants to make us grow and become stronger with power. … The word for power is the Greek word "dunamis" which means, "infused strength, physical or moral." It is the same miracle power that God used to raise Jesus from the dead. We derive the word dynamite from the Greek word dunamis. God wants to make us stronger using dunamis power through His Spirit in our inner man…[22]

Jesus didn't strive. He found his power reignited through times of prayer with His Father. He found time to delight in relationships with those He came in contact with. He found delight in community and in ministering to those around Him. He

---

[21] John Gill's Exposition of the Bible is in the public domain and may be freely used and distributed. Found at:<http://www.biblestudytools.com/commentaries/gills-exposition-of-the-bible/ephesians-3//>

[22] Wickstrom Stephen P. "Bible study on Paul's Prayer". Used by permission. Found at spwbooks @spwickstrom.com.

found joy in giving of Himself to make life abundant for others.

- *Knowing that God's unlimited resources strengthen me* helps me to stop striving to accomplish my agenda and instead to seek to know His.

- *Knowing that God's unlimited resources strengthen me* leads me to realize my neediness of knowing Him more.

- *Knowing that God's unlimited resources strengthen me* leads me to seek greater dependence on Him through prayer.

God's power raised Christ from the dead to make real for us the promise of salvation. His death and resurrection touched the whole world giving us hope for eternity. He embraced others by healing them physically, emotionally and spiritually. He is faithful. *Surely goodness and lovingkindness will follow me all the days of my life.*

2. Growing a heart for Sabbath rest requires us to know God's marvelous love.

Again, we return to Paul's prayer. In Ephesians 3:17-19 (AMP), Paul says:

"May Christ through your faith [actually] dwell (settle down, abide, make His permanent home) in your hearts! May you be rooted deep in love *and* founded securely on love. That you may have the power and be strong to apprehend *and* grasp with all the saints [God's devoted people, the experience of that love] what is the breadth and length and height and depth [of it]. [That you may really come] to know [practically, through experience for yourselves] the love of Christ, which far surpasses mere knowledge [without experience] that you may be filled [through all your being] unto all the fullness of God [may have the richest measure of the divine Presence, and become a body wholly filled and flooded with God Himself]!"

God's love in good times and in the difficult times help us to learn that it is safe to rest in Him and resting in Him helps us to know more of His presence in our lives:

> Love should be rooted and grounded, thoroughly fixed in our minds so as to resemble a well founded building – a deeply planted tree. Our roots ought to be so deeply planted and our foundation so firmly laid that nothing will be able to shake us.[23]

He is our all-satisfying God no matter what the circumstance. He is the God of extravagant love. I express this *extravagant love* in the following poem that I wrote.

---

[23] Calvin, John. "John Calvin's Commentary on Galatians and Ephesians" is public domain and may be freely used and distributed. Found at:
http://www.ccel.org/ccel/calvin/comm.vol141/htm/About.htm

Extravagant

How extravagant the love
The perfume poured out
She anointed His body
Others indignant gave shout

How extravagant the love
His body the jar
Was broken and emptied
Redemption's plan from afar

How extravagant the love
Blood cleanses our sin
He sacrificed it all
And our salvation did win

How extravagant the love
Fragrance from heaven
We now are the vessels
To share what He has given

How extravagant the love
Poured into my heart
His Spirit resides there
For me His truths to impart

How extravagant the love
He has given me

To bear witness to Him
To His grace and His glory

God's love in Christ, that extravagant love helps us through all of life's ups-and-downs. His love helps us to keep an eternal perspective. Focusing on eternity helps us to better discern what is important in the here and now. We can choose to give of our time and money, or share our talents in helping others with a spirit of generosity. We remember what really matters, that we are to store up treasures in heaven (see Matthew 6:20).

- *Knowing His love* can help us to let go of the control and keep God in His rightful place as the sovereign One.

- *Knowing His love* helps us to honor Him and rejoice in His presence because of the relationship we share.

- *Knowing His love* can lead us to want to know Him more.

- *Knowing His love* gives us a joyful heart, which spills over in our lives in response to others.

3. *Growing a heart for Sabbath rest requires us to recognize that God through His mighty power working in us is able to accomplish (carry out His purpose) infinitely more than we can ask or imagine.*

Once again, we go back to Paul's prayer, Ephesians 3:20 (AMP) says:

> "Now to Him Who, by (in consequence of) the [action of His] power that is at work within us, is able to [carry out His purpose and] do superabundantly, far over *and* above all that we [dare} ask or think [infinitely beyond our highest prayers, desires, thoughts, hopes or dreams]."

The Lord's power demonstrated in and through us, and His grace, love and power manifested to us should be faith-building. It should grow in us a stronger confidence for that which is yet to come. John Calvin explains that what "Exceedingly abundantly above all that we ask or think" really means is, "Whatever expectations we form of Divine blessings the infinite goodness of God will exceed all our wishes and all our thoughts." We will always be amazed at how good, how great the blessings and goodness of God.

Steven Wickstrom explains the Lord's power as follows:

. . . Now to Him that is able (can do) to do far more abundantly above all we ask or think. The word abundantly is not in the original Greek, it was added in by the translators of the NASB for clarity. The words far more is the Greek word "*huperekperissou*" which means, superabundantly, beyond all measure. God is able to do over, above and beyond all that we ask or even think. This takes us into a whole new realm of understanding of God. God can go beyond what we even think about asking but do not ask for. The things we do not even think of, He can do for us. What an awesome God we serve! How often do we not ask God to do something because we do not think that he can do it? This verse continues with, according (agreeing with, in harmony with) to the power (*dunamis*) that works (Greek word "*energeo*" which means, to be active, to operate) in us. When we paraphrase this verse back together again, it reads: 'Now unto Him (God the Father) who can do over, above, and beyond all we ask or think, in agreement and in harmony with the strengthening power (by becoming infused with God) that actively operates in us . . . [24]

God empowers you to fulfill His purpose and enables you to do His will. Have you tapped into His power and strength?

- *Knowing that He can do for us more abundantly above all we ask or think* helps us to set aside work.

- *Knowing that He can do for us more abundantly above all we ask or think* helps us to trust Him to help us accomplish His

---

[24] Wickstrom, Steven P. "Bible Study on Paul's Prayer." Used by permission. Found at: spwbooks@spwickstrom.com

purpose in us.

- *Knowing that He can do for us more abundantly above all we ask or think* leads us to have a thankful heart as we realize all that He has done and is doing in our lives.

- *Knowing that He can do for us more abundantly above all we ask or think* means we can be satisfied with what He has given us and stop looking for more of what this world has to offer.

- *Knowing that He can do for us more abundantly above all we ask or think* helps us to pour out our hearts and wait on Him rather than to take matters into our own hands, manipulating circumstances.

The Lord calls us to rest in Him and to take time apart in our lives to honor the Sabbath and keep it holy. He created the world in six days and then He rested on the seventh day. We are made in His image and He desires us to know this rhythm of work and rest, also.

We see from the beginning all the way back in the book of Genesis how our God created a world and desired relationship with the men and women He created. Before the fall of man, Adam and Eve lived in perfect fellowship with God. Throughout the Bible, we read of how God seeks relationship with us and how men and women of God seek His presence. Like David desired to feast on God's faithfulness and bask in the presence of God. We too need to make time to be with God as we live here on this earth and yearn as David did to dwell with Him in heaven. Don't we hear that desire in David in his future hope of *dwelling in the house of the Lord forever*? He desires to be with the Lord, in His presence.

As we choose to spend time with our God delighting in His presence we come to know more of who He is, and how He touches our lives with His attributes and character. As we seek to be in His presence, to know Him more, we find that our knowing Him comes in times of solitude as we seek Him in prayer, in our personal Bible reading/Bible study as well as in time of corporate worship with our Christian community. Sabbath-keeping offers us extended time to delight in relationships of those around us, to seek deeper intimacy and to demonstrate hospitality. We have time to show our love, to talk together, to pray together, to be present rather than always busy doing.

In reaching for God's presence, I am learning how well He knows my heart and my needs because I am experiencing how He meets me in them. He meets my needs for fun, for connection, and for love in different ways and always leads me to come away rejoicing.

We are called to "…walk (live and conduct ourselves) in a manner worthy of the Lord, fully pleasing to Him *and* desiring to please Him in all things, bearing fruit in every good work and steadily growing *and* increasing in *and* by the knowledge of God [with fuller, deeper and clearer insight, acquaintance and recognition]" Colossians 1:10 (AMP). We are free to live out our anointing in however the Holy Spirit leads as we enjoy the gifts He has so richly bestowed on us. We are free to live out Sabbath rest and come to know more of His presence. We are free to live out Sabbath rest and in doing so we learn more of what David longed for, *to dwell with the Lord forever.*

In this life, we move from the wilderness of hopelessness to worship of the one who is our Eternal Hope. We move from the wilderness of restlessness, and desperateness to the worship of Him whose presence is all-satisfying to us. We move from the wilderness of this earthly dwelling to live in constant worship in heaven.

Questions:
For Life Application

1. How has the Lord taught you of His mercy in your life?

2. As you ponder the magnitude of the God's love in the spiritual blessings He bestows on us, how will you respond? Are you moved to worship?

3. How will you come to know more of God's presence in your days?

4. Describe why rest fills your heart and soul as you read Ephesians 3:16-20? What do these verses mean to you?

APPENDIX:

Our thoughts tell us a lot about the lies we believe. How do your thoughts compare to what God's Word says? Here are some thoughts that may go through your mind followed by what the Word of God says regarding this.

Human Thoughts say: It's okay to tell this little secret about her; She'll never know. I don't like him, he makes me so mad, he did this and this…

God's Word says: "Let no unwholesome word proceed from your mouth, but only such a word as is good for edification according to the need of the moment, so that it will give grace to those who hear." (Ephesians 4:29)

Human Thoughts say: My boss is mean to me, he expects way too much of me, forget him, I'll show him, I'm not working today.

God's Word says: "Slaves, in all things obey those who are your masters on earth, not with external service, as those who merely please men, but with sincerity of heart, fearing the Lord. Whatever you do, do your work heartily, as for the Lord rather than for men…" (Colossians 3:22-23)

Human Thoughts say: I don't need to go to church today I need some extra sleep, besides I read my Bible everyday this week.

God's Words says: "and let us consider how to stimulate one another to love and good deeds, not forsaking our own assembling together, as is the habit of some, but encouraging one another; and all the more as you see the day drawing near..." (Hebrews 10:24-25)

Human Thoughts say: It's hopeless, I'm hopeless, there is no help for me, and I may as well just kill myself.

God's Word says: "Therefore let us draw near with confidence to the throne of grace, so that we may receive mercy and find grace to help in time of need." (Hebrews 4:16)

Human Thoughts say: I feel so all alone, no one really cares about me.

God's Word says: "I WILL NEVER DESERT YOU, NOR WILL I EVER FORSAKE YOU,"(Hebrews 13:5b)

Human Thoughts say: Oh, this little thing doesn't matter other people do a lot worse things than this.

God's Word says: "Therefore, since we have so great a cloud of witnesses surrounding us, let us also lay aside every encumbrance and the sin which so easily entangles us, and let us run with endurance the race that is set before us, fixing our eyes on Jesus, the author and perfecter of faith, who for the joy set before Him endured the cross, despising the shame, and has sat down at the right hand of the throne of God. For consider Him who has endured such hostility by sinners against Himself, so that you will not grow weary and lose heart." (Hebrews 12:1-3)

Human Thoughts say: I just don't know what to do – this problem seems so impossible, who can I call? Who should I ask?

God's Word says: "But if any of you lacks wisdom, let him ask of God, who gives to all generously and without reproach, and it will be given to him." (James 1:5)

Human Thoughts say: Ugh, why pray, it doesn't do any good anyway, God never answers my prayer.

God's Word says: "Cast your burden upon the LORD and He will sustain you; He will never allow the righteous to be shaken." (Psalm 55:22)

"The effective prayer of a righteous man can accomplish much." (James 5:16b)

Human Thoughts say: I can wear this, it looks good, and it's what everyone is wearing.

God's Word says; "Your adornment must not be merely external— braiding the hair, and wearing gold jewelry, or putting on dresses; but let it be the hidden person of the heart, with the

154

imperishable quality of a gentle and quiet spirit, which is precious in the sight of God." (1 Peter 3:3-4)

Human Thoughts say: ANGRY WORDS

God's Word says: "Set a guard, O LORD, over my mouth; Keep watch over the door of my lips." (Psalm 141:3)

"Let your speech always be with grace, as though seasoned with salt, so that you will know how you should respond to each person." (Colossians 4:6)

Human Thoughts say: It doesn't matter if I go the speed limit.

God's Word says: "Submit yourselves for the Lord's sake to every human institution, whether to a king as the one in authority, or to governors as sent by him for the punishment of evildoers and the praise of those who do right. For such is the will of God that by doing right you may silence the ignorance of foolish men." (1 Peter 2:13-15)

Human Thoughts say: Ugh, this is hopeless, I am so bad, I can never stop this, it is impossible, I am stuck, and I am always so tempted and give into this.

God's Word says: "...then the Lord knows how to rescue the godly from temptation, and to keep the unrighteous under punishment for the day of judgment . . ." (2 Peter 2:9)

Human Thoughts say: This is mine, I earned this money and I can use it for me, how I want to.

God's Word says: "Every good thing given and every perfect gift is from above, coming down from the Father of lights, with whom there is no variation or shifting shadow." (James 1:17)

Human Thoughts say: OOOH, I am so good, I am… I do… I can… I will.

God's Word says: "Therefore humble yourselves under the mighty hand of God, that He may exalt you at the proper time," (1 Peter 5:6)

Human Thoughts say: I don't belong.

God's Word says: "Bless our God, O peoples, And sound His praise abroad, Who keeps us in life And does not allow our feet to slip." (Psalm 66:8-9)

RECOMMENDED READINGS:

Briscoe, Pete and Hickman, Patricia. *Secrets from the Treadmill.* Nelson Books 2004

Buchanan, Mark. *The Rest of God; Restoring Your Soul by Restoring Sabbath,* Thomas Nelson 2006.

Card, Michael. *A Sacred Sorrow.* Navpress 2005.

Kent, Keri Wyatt. *Rest: Living in Sabbath Simplicity.* Zondervan 2009.

Franklin, Jentezen, *Fasting.* Charisma House; December 2007

Lawrence, Brother and Laubach, Frank. *Practicing His Presence.* Gene Edward ©MCMLXXIII.

Lucado, Max. *Safe in the Shepherd's Arms: Hope and Encouragement from Psalm 23.* Thomas Nelson 2002.

McHenry, Janet Holm. *PrayerStreaming.* WaterBrook Press 2005.

Olford, Stephen F. *Not I but CHRIST.* Christian Focus Publications 1995.

Piper, John. *A Hunger for God.* Crossway Books. 1997.

Reeve, Pamela. *Deserts of the Heart: Finding God during the Dry Times.* Multnomah Publishers 2000.

Smith, Hannah Whitall. *The God of All Comfort.* Ballantine Books 1986.

Thrasher, Bill. *A Journey to Victorious Praying.* Moody Publishers, 2003

**"This is my comfort in my affliction,
That Your word has revived me."**
Psalm 119:50

Personal Notes

Personal Notes

Personal Notes

A Note from the Author:

I hope that this book has touched your heart and drawn you into deeper intimacy with the Lord. It is going through the dark times, the wilderness times in life that we find the Refuge that our Lord God truly is. It is in continually seeking Him in the midst of our pain that we come to know His love, compassion, mercy and healing. It is when we truly depend upon Him and nothing of our own.

As you continue your journey through life, through the mountaintop experiences, and the wilderness times, I pray that you know His presence with you. Look for Him at every turn, seek His face, and listen to His voice.

May you know the joy of journeying with the Shepherd.

Cheryl Gerou

If you are struggling through a personal wilderness, I would love to pray for you. Please send me an email letting me know specifically how I can pray for you.

Send your email to: fromwildernesstoworship@gmail.com

Believers Prayer

Dear Reader,

If you do not know the Lord as your personal Savior, and want to come to know Him, you can start right now by praying a simple prayer to Him. This is just an example, use your own words, He wants to hear it from your heart.

Lord Jesus, I do not know you. I have heard of you and read of you, now I realize I need a personal relationship with you. Thank you so much for dying on the cross for my sins. I want you to come into my life. I need you to take full control of my life. I ask you now to be my Savior and the Lord of my life. Thank you for granting me forgiveness for my sins and offering eternal life to me. I accept your forgiveness, and now, I desire for you to make me into the person you desire for me to be. Help me learn of you and grow in relationship with you. In your holy name, I pray. Amen.

The Lord rejoices in all who come to believe in Him. Continue to seek Him in prayer, pour your heart out to Him. You will want to get a Bible to lead you in knowing more about our Savior. You will also want to find a Bible-believing church to attend. Let the pastor know that you are a new believer so that he can help you in learning to study the Word.

May the Lord bless you as you learn to walk more closely with Him each day.

www.ingramcontent.com/pod-product-compliance
Lightning Source LLC
LaVergne TN
LVHW021448080426
835509LV00018B/2204